D1440465

# GAMECHANGER
## *SPENCER FC*

EBURY
PRESS

1 3 5 7 9 10 8 6 4 2

Ebury Press, an imprint of Ebury Publishing
20 Vauxhall Bridge Road
London SW1V 2SA

Ebury Press is part of the Penguin Random House group of
companies whose addresses can be found at
global.penguinrandomhouse.com

Penguin
Random House
UK

First published by Ebury Press in 2017
This edition published in 2018

www.penguin.co.uk

A CIP catalogue record for this book is available from the
British Library

ISBN 9781785039836

Typeset in 10.35/19.32 pt ITC Galliard Std
by Integra Software Services Pvt. Ltd, Pondicherry

Printed and bound in Great Britain by Clays Ltd, Elcograf S.p.A.

MIX
Paper from
responsible sources
FSC® C018179

Penguin Random House is committed to a
sustainable future for our business, our readers
and our planet. This book is made from Forest
Stewardship Council® certified paper.

# CONTENTS

# KICK-OFF: THE MAGIC OF THE WEMBLEY CUP

I stormed down the tunnel with the roar of the crowd still ringing in my ears. It was all square at 3–3 against Weller Wanderers in the 2016 Wembley Cup final. This was supposed to be our big day at Wembley, our Champions League final – the biggest match of our lives – but we'd played like we were strangers so far and I wasn't happy with the way things had been going at all.

I was fuming as I got to the dressing room, but our manager, Arsenal legend Martin Keown, pulled me to one side and said, 'Spence, don't go in there angry. We're riding a wave after fighting back from 3–1 down so you've got to keep it super-positive in there with the team.'

He was right. And with 20,000 people watching in the stands and millions more on YouTube, we knew we had to up our game for the fans. We came out full of intent in the second half ... only to go 4–3 down to a goal from Wanderers forward Theo Baker.

I looked across at my teammates, at legends like Jamie Carragher, Patrick Kluivert and Robert Pirès, at freestyler forward Daniel Cutting who was desperate to score, and at my own brother Seb, such a strong competitor, and I knew we had it in our locker to turn this around. 'Come on, boys!' I shouted.

In the 63rd minute Robert Pirès went tearing into the box, as he had on so many occasions for Arsenal in the Premier League, and squared the ball for ChuBoi to put an easy finish past the keeper. We were back in it, and when that man ChuBoi won a penalty for us only six minutes later we had an opportunity to take the lead.

There was only one man for the job in my eyes: Seb.

It's difficult to describe just how loud it is playing in front of a crowd of thousands of people at the home of football. You have to shout at the top of your voice just to even attempt to be heard, and my voice was already hoarse. But at that moment, in the hush that descended as Seb stepped up to take his penalty, you could have heard a pin drop. The tension was unbearable, but Seb remained cool to the last. He wrong-footed the keeper and slotted it effortlessly into the back of the net. Get in! I ran straight to the corner for Seb's trademark golf celebration: he mimed putting a ball into the hole where I was playing caddie with the flag.

As children, we'd kicked a ball about in the back garden with each other, pretending we were playing at Wembley for England or West Ham. For both of us to be playing in the same team, celebrating his goal, at the real Wembley Stadium was beyond our wildest dreams.

But we still had a job to do. With our defence expertly marshalled by Jamie Carragher, our forwards had the freedom to attack, and we kept the pressure on Wanderers. Manny made it six for us and then Daniel Cutting finally got his Wembley goal to put us 7–4 ahead after a superb run from Séan Garnier. Surely the game was ours now, but I didn't dare contemplate it. We needed to keep cool heads until ...

The final whistle blew. I couldn't believe it. We'd done it – we'd won the Wembley Cup for the second year running! We'd fought back from 3–1 down to an unbelievable victory! The crowd roared its approval, and every moment felt like I was walking through the dream I'd spent most of my life practising for.

I collected my winners' medal from our manager Martin Keown, and then, as team captain, I took my place at the centre of the winners' podium, with friends, family and football legends – my teammates – either side of me. I grinned at the camera and to all the people watching at home, with my hands hovering above the trophy, before I lifted it triumphantly above my head, just as I'd seen so many FA Cup, World Cup and Champions League winners do on TV. The fireworks went off with a bang, the flamethrowers lit up, the glitter cannons rained the shiny stuff down on us and we all started jumping up and down as the celebrations began. It was every bit as crazy and awesome as I'd ever hoped for.

It was quite simply the best moment of my life.

So, how on earth did this happen? How did a kid who at one point couldn't even get in his school team end up playing at Wembley Stadium in front of 20,000 people? How did someone who spent his life playing computer games and making YouTube videos get to play football in the same side as World Cup- and Champions League-winning players?

How did the creator of a YouTube channel write an introduction to his book that reads like the start of a professional footballer's memoir?

I'm part of a growing movement of people who, despite fervently supporting a Premier League team and loving the sport at the top level, want more from the game than what the Football Association and FIFA serve up. With my YouTube channel Spencer FC and my Hashtag United team I'm a football club owner outside the traditional football structure. I'm putting out football matches that are drawing audiences bigger than many professional clubs, and I've been lucky enough to do that alongside the great friends and family I've played football with for decades.

I'm doing it because I love it. I love video games, I love making YouTube content and I live and breathe this beautiful game of ours. In our community – the world that millions of YouTube creators and viewers inhabit – we connect the dots between all of this and engage with the game and the audience in ways unlike anyone has before.

As my Twitter bio reads, life's a game called football and I intend to play it. Over the last few years I've changed the game so I can play by my own rules and map out my own road to Wembley. This is how I did it . . .

# 1

# 'COULD HAVE BEEN GREAT
# AT SNOOKER'

Alright, mate, how you doing? Welcome to my story, and like any good story, it makes sense to start at the beginning.

Believe it or not, I wasn't always football mad. In fact, it really amazes some people considering how much my life revolves around it now that I didn't really get into football properly until I was 12 or 13 years old. If you compare that with my older brother Seb, who was obsessed by the time he was 5, playing at a very high level and smashing it by the time he was 12, you can see I had a lot of catching up to do.

My dad, a lifelong West Ham supporter, did his best to get me into it, of course. He took me, Seb and my younger brother Saunders to West Ham games, and I loved going to Upton Park – it was a great day out with the family, with the roar of the crowd and the kind of cheeky language on the terraces you definitely didn't hear at home – but I had no urge to watch the game on TV, let alone play it. I just wasn't that bothered about it.

But that all changed for me massively during 1998, which was a big year for football: firstly, it was the World Cup in France, and secondly, it was the year I properly got into the video game *FIFA: Road to World Cup 98*.

I watched the England games during the World Cup with my family, and we'd all gather round the TV and cheer the lads on – legends like Tony Adams, Alan Shearer, David Beckham and Michael Owen. When England played Argentina in the last 16 of the tournament, we were all perched on the edge of my mum and dad's bed going mad at the game. Michael Owen gave us all hope with an unbelievable goal – that was his special moment and I idolised him for it (I also kind of loved that his surname was the same as my middle name) – and then came Beckham's kick on Diego Simeone … oh no! Becks was sent off but England were brilliant, fighting for everything and drawing the game 2–2. But when they went out on the dreaded penalties, I was in tears. So much for not being bothered.

Moments like this started to add up (not always with tears, of course), and then there was *FIFA 98*. I'd played video games before, things like *Mario Kart* and *GoldenEye,* but playing *FIFA* with Seb was the next level.

We'd play the game against each other in two-player mode on the PC, long before you could compete online, and Seb would use the keyboard and I'd have the mouse. It was basically a stitch-up, as it was close to impossible to win on the mouse. You had to physically move the mouse to move the player, so I'd move the mouse one way to move my player ... and whack into the keyboard. I'd go the other, and the mouse would go off the desk. Seb was better than me by a million miles anyway, so I didn't stand a chance. But it didn't put me off. I loved it, and I kept chipping away, playing and losing all the time but slowly getting better. What's the old phrase, 'You either win or you learn'? Well, I guess in this case you could say Seb well and truly took me to school.

*FIFA* inevitably led to *Football Manager* (which was called *Championship Manager* back then), and that's where I started getting properly hooked. It's difficult to play *Football Manager* without an obsessive streak, and it takes over lives – I'd come home from school and go straight upstairs to play it for hours on end. But the thing about *Football Manager* is that it's a singular obsession. You get so invested in it, and it means so much to you, but you could turn to the person sitting next to you at school, who is just as much a *Football Manager* nut as you, and say, 'Mate, you don't understand. Batistuta scored thirty goals for me in my first season, but then I got in this other guy and he scored forty – it was amazing!'

And this person will just say, 'Sweet, mate.'

He doesn't care at all. He's not invested in your game like you. He'll tell you about his own game and you'll be rolling your eyes and saying, 'Sweet, mate,' too. The internet has changed all this now, obviously, but back then the life of a *Football Manager* obsessive could be a lonely one.

When I started secondary school, it was at a different school to the one most of my mates were going to. They went to the private school nearby, while I did my 11-plus exams and applied to a couple of really good grammar schools in the Essex area, one called KEGS (King Edward VI Grammar School) – up there with the best in the country and closest to home – and another called Westcliff, which was bloody miles away. I ended up at Westcliff.

For the first few years of secondary school I was up at six o'clock in the morning to catch a bus that basically took the scenic route around the whole of Essex so I could get to Westcliff. Added to the fact that I was a bit gutted to be going to this school without any of my mates there, I didn't take to things very quickly. At the end of my first week, my mum asked, 'How's school going? Have you made any friends?'

I said, 'Yeah, I have. There's this one guy, he's a really good lad. I always have a good chat with him and we spend a lot of time together.'

'Oh, yes. What's his name?' said Mum. 'His name's Bob,' I replied. 'He's the bus driver.'

We laugh about this now, but back then, while it might be a bit hard to believe, I wasn't always the chatty, confident guy you see on YouTube. I've always been a bit of an attention-seeker – call it middle-child syndrome if you like – and I loved doing school plays and things like that. I was a bit of a geek too, into things like Warhammer and joining the school quiz team, but I struggled at first with being the new boy. Football would change all that.

Playing *Football Manager* had given me an education into the game, all the teams, the players, the stats – the amount of information you can absorb in football is crazy – but now I wanted to play the game in real life too.

One thing I've had throughout my whole life is a good attitude. When I get into something, I always give it my best. Now, that's great, but at some point you have to get some ability, right? Coming to football so late meant I really didn't have any, so I thought to myself, *I'm going to catch up – I'm going to get as good as the other guys.*

If you've ever read a footballer's autobiography by someone like Wayne Rooney, who talks about obsessively kicking a ball against the wall of his grandmother's house when he was a kid, imagine an unbelievably bad version of that and you're still not close to where I started in my back garden.

Gradually, I found a group of mates to play football with at lunchtime. In English lessons, I'd scribble down England XIs or Premier League XIs in my rough book with the lad sitting next to me. All we talked about was football. Things changed at home, too. Seb and I hadn't got on all that well as kids, but football started to bring us closer together, even if there was still a huge gap in our skill levels, and we started to bond and become really close friends.

By this stage, I was hooked on football – but I wasn't satisfied. Playing at lunchtime or in the garden was fun, but I wanted a more competitive opportunity. I needed to join a Sunday team. After an unsuccessful trial with Seb's team, Brentwood Boys, I eventually started playing for a club called Hartswood Stars. By 'playing', I mean mostly training and watching from the sidelines. I think in two seasons with Hartswood Stars I might have started just three games. It was slow progress.

When I was 14 we moved house. We relocated from Brentwood to a small village near Chelmsford called Little Baddow, so I needed a new club (probably for the best – if this had been *Football Manager* then the virtual me would have handed in a transfer request a long time ago on account of not getting enough game time!). There was a local team called Heybridge Swifts. The men's side were a good team, semi-pro, but the kids', well, they were a bit more average – which meant I had a chance.

I was the new boy once again. I was nervous at first, worrying about whether the other kids would like me, though mainly I was worrying about whether I'd get in the team. I needn't have worried about the latter, as I got in the team quite quickly because the manager loved me for my good attitude (I was super-keen) and the fact that I was never late to training.

I was right to worry about the former, though, as I don't think the other kids in the team particularly liked me. Not because I was a bad kid or anything, but it was more that they all went to the same school and knew each other from there. I was quiet and shy at the time, certainly in the football world. They would have been shocked if they'd known I loved performing in school plays.

There was another reason, aside from my attitude, that helped me get into the starting line-up. At that age, the one thing no one was really doing was heading the ball properly. A huge, up-and-under goal kick? Forget it – few 14-year-olds fancied planting their head on the end of one of them. So I saw an opportunity. I was playing left-back at the time – a position people aren't exactly queuing up to play – and I'd make sure I got up into the centre circle and headed the ball back each time. I was tall for my age, which meant few people had a chance of beating me in the air, and this made me invaluable to my team. I'd practise at home, too, and I'd even score a few headers as I improved. But my feet, well, my feet were terrible.

Being stuck out at left-back meant I was in the position where I could do the least amount of damage possible, which was just as well because I was right-footed. Playing there slowly but surely improved my left foot, however, which meant that eventually I could claim to be two-footed, just as long as you understand that meant I was equally bad with both feet.

Now, when I talk about this team being 'local', what I actually mean is they were an eight-mile bicycle ride away. My mum and dad worked long hours while my brothers and I were kids, so they weren't usually around to give me a lift to training, but I didn't care. Football was my entire world by this stage, and I would cycle eight miles there after school and I'd get the bus home with my bike when it was too dark later on.

One evening after school, I was cycling to training on the pavement when my wheels locked and I suddenly skidded and went flying off onto the road, straight in front of a car. The car only clipped my wheel, but it sent me into the path of another vehicle. My heart was in my mouth for a split second, time seemed to stop ... before I went over the bonnet and crashed to the ground.

I was unbelievably lucky, not that you'd have thought it if you'd seen the state of me. I gingerly got to my feet, trembling and with blood streaming down the side of my head and pouring from my knee, gravel-marks peppering my legs. My bike was in a sorry state too, in a crumpled heap by the kerb with the front wheel bent and buckled.

The driver got out of his car and came running up to me. 'Are you OK?' he asked, his eyes wild with panic. 'Do you want me to ring an ambulance?'

I only had one thought in my head, though.

'I'm going to be late for training,' I said to the guy, who looked dumbstruck. I was only about a mile away, so I grabbed my bike, which was totally unrideable, and just threw it over my shoulder and ran the rest of the way to training.

I staggered into training ten minutes late – I'd never been late before – and all I could think was, I'm not going to play at the weekend now because I'm late. As soon as I saw Sean, the manager, I said, 'Sean, I'm really sorry ... '

Sean looked only a little less unsettled than the driver that hit me as he surveyed my battle damage. 'What the hell happened to you?'

'I got hit by a car,' I said, gasping to catch my breath, 'but it's OK, I'm here now. I can still play.'

After giving me a once-over, Sean realised that somehow I'd managed to avoid any long-term injury, and rather than worrying about the state of mind of a blood-soaked left-back declaring himself fit for training, Sean was impressed by my attitude. So impressed, in fact, that the following week he decided to make me captain of the team.

Now, being captain of a football team at any level demands certain qualities. A talkative captain can inspire his teammates with bold words, and if you're not the most vocal player you can lead by example, though then you probably need to be the best player. I wasn't the most vocal, as I was still the new kid in this group and we weren't friends outside the team, and I definitely wasn't the best player. I just had the best attitude, and that's not enough, in my opinion. You need a bit more than that, and so it proved as I found out the hard way.

The other kids hated the fact that I was captain, so about halfway through the season the captaincy was quietly moved on to another player. I wasn't sorry to lose it, and nor were the other players. It was a nice gesture from the manager making me captain, and he would go on to name me Manager's Player of the Year a couple of times for the team. I never won the Players' Player, of course. That goes to the best player. Being popular never hurts either.

I did get a lot better, though, and I would eventually fully justify my place in the team. The key to this was very simple. I'd go out into the back garden again and again, on my own, and just practise. When I wanted to get better at slide tackling, I'd go out there and kick the ball in front of me and then slide tackle the ball against one of the most accommodating opponents there is: thin air.

Once I turned 15, the next step was trying to get into the school team, which was a much higher level of football. After seeing that I was one of the better players in the air, Mr Williams, our PE teacher who ran the team, attempted to try to turn me into a target man. For some reason our year group lacked strikers, and so they tried to fit a round peg into a square hole. I was playing left-back on Sundays and up front for my school in the week. Needless to say, I don't think I ever scored a goal for Westcliff, and even though I may have notched up a few cheeky assists, the experiment would go down as a failure. I definitely wasn't a striker.

As I approached the end of Year 11, Seb had gone to university and my younger brother Saunders wasn't into football – he loves it now, but he wouldn't get into it until he went to university himself, where he had even more catching up to do than I did. I would come home from school and say, 'Saunders, come and play football with me in the garden,' and he rarely wanted to. He was massively into his music and was usually playing the drums or mastering some other instrument, so I'd be off to practise rabonas or penalty kicks against thin air once again.

I was obsessed, and when I wasn't playing football I was playing football video games. By this point Seb and I had moved on to the *Pro Evolution Soccer* series of games.

I never really beat Seb at *PES* until I was 15, and even then we'd play 30-game marathon sessions and I'd maybe win two or three games. We could never end on me winning, though. If I beat him there'd always be one more to play. Older brother's prerogative, I suppose.

Over the course of Seb heading off to uni, where he played lots of *PES* with his mates, and my doing the same a few years later, I eventually got better than him at the game, and when we played I'd smash him every time. And what happened then? Seb didn't want to play any more. I couldn't believe it. 'What do you mean?' I'd say. 'I've stuck it out for the best part of a decade losing to you, using the mouse while you had the keyboard on *FIFA,* which is what's motivated me to get so good, and now you don't want to play any more?'

That's right: he didn't. He saw himself as a winner and that's all he likes to remind me about now, his hammering me game after game when we were kids – even though I beat him every time when we play *FIFA* on my channel now!

Back at school, I was still going at it on *Football Manager,* too, not that anyone cared outside my little bubble of a bedroom. Oddly enough, I always had a little niggling thought at the back of my mind when I'd play: *What am I doing? Why am I spending all of this time on something that won't lead anywhere?*

I'm a pretty efficient guy – always have been. It's why I've never really got into playing golf. Seb loves it, but I'd rather play a couple of games of football or really smash it on the squash court, have some full-on exercise, burn some calories and then get on with my day. I was the same as a kid – except when it came to video games.

I wouldn't have let myself do anything else that had no real end point to it, but still I would allow hours and hours of my day to be sucked up by football games. *Football Manager* is a black hole where time is concerned – a thrillingly magnetic one too, of course – but the way I like to justify it these days is to think about the game as a metaphor for life: You can work hard at it and win the Champions League ten seasons in a row, but one day your game's going to freeze and you'll never play it again, and you'll ask yourself, 'What was it all for?'

So you can either do it to the best of your ability and absolutely smash it, even though one day it will be over and no one will even care, or you can just not bother. And that's how I feel about life.

Of course, this kind of philosophical reasoning didn't exactly wash with my mum and dad. They never tired of telling me that I was wasting my time playing video games, and if I ever misbehaved they confiscated the games as a punishment.

What none of us realised at the time, though, was that playing these games was actually super-valuable: all those hours spent on *FIFA, PES* and *Football Manager* were just preparing me for my job. Without that time spent playing those games just for the love of it – no one dreamed of making a living from their own YouTube channel back then because it just wasn't an option – I wouldn't have been able to do what I do today.

While Mum and Dad might not have been too encouraging when it came to video games, they certainly instilled a strong work ethic and competitive nature in me and my brothers. Both my parents worked long hours. My dad ran his own business doing refrigeration and air-conditioning installation, while my mum worked at Ford Motor Company.

Dad started from nothing, really, and he began his career as a British Gas apprentice, but he was destined to be his own boss. Even while working as an apprentice he was running his own burger van in the evenings. He's had a number of different businesses throughout his life, and he's never been scared to try something new or back himself. His entrepreneurial spirit meant that I didn't grow up thinking I had to follow a clear path from school to university and get a 'solid' job like a doctor or lawyer. Dad's example meant that I knew I didn't have to just accept the status quo and do what everyone, including the teachers at school, tells you to do. I knew I didn't have to follow the crowd.

Many years later, in 2013, I went to the FIFA Interactive World Cup in Madrid, which is basically the World Cup for the *FIFA* video game. I wasn't there as a competitor

(I'm a good player, but I'm definitely not a pro-level player). I was there more as a type of journalist, I suppose.

While I was there, I played a one-off game against Alfonso Ramos from Spain, a guy who was, at the time, the only person to have won the tournament twice. A two-times world champion. Before we played I challenged him by saying,

'If I beat you, you have to give me your World Cup-winning shirt and sign it saying I'm better than you.'

He agreed ... and I won the game! I beat the world champion thanks to an Andy Carroll goal – the West Ham connection seeing me to the biggest *FIFA* victory of my life. I couldn't believe it. Alfonso was as good as his word, and he sent me his shirt on which he had written: 'You're the best *FIFA* player in the world.' It was an amazing moment for me, and it somehow seemed to make sense of all that time I'd spent playing the game as a kid.

I couldn't wait to tell my dad after the game, and I texted him straight away: 'I've just beaten the world champion at *FIFA*. So much for a wasted childhood, eh?!'

It didn't take long for Dad to reply.

'Well done,' he said, 'but with all that time you could have been great at snooker.' I think that's what they call a generational divide.

• • •

I got my first taste of internet fame when I was at school – and it had nothing to do with football. I started filming music videos of myself miming to pop hits in my mum and dad's attic. Some were funny, or at least I think they were, and some were just pure cringe. When I showed my mate Pete some of them when he was round at my house, he said, 'Can you send me them on MSN?' (This was way before WhatsApp. Back then, MSN was the place to be to chat with your mates after school.)

I should have sensed a stitch-up a mile off, but instead I sent them to him in good faith and pure naivety. And he went and uploaded them to the internet. Cheers, Pete! One of them, my rendition of 'Don't Stop Me Now' by Queen, went viral and got something like 600,000 views (this was a lot back then) on Google Video (the precursor to YouTube). Featuring me topless and my super-skinny teenage frame on display, this video was definitely not meant for public consumption.

It got played in school assembly, much to my horror, and someone even came up to me when I was playing snooker in Chelmsford and said, 'You're the kid from "Don't Stop Me Now".'

Yet another reason why greatness at snooker was always likely to elude me.

# 2

## STAND-UP GUY

Since my obsession with the game began, I always wanted to start a football club. Now, that's a lofty ambition in anyone's eyes, I know, but after I sat my GCSEs in 2005 and school was out for summer, my time playing for Heybridge came to an end. A lot of youth football teams finish when the players turn 16, and Heybridge was no different. It means a lot of lads often stop playing the game for good at this time too.

Not me though. My only thought was: *No way am I stopping playing football – I've only just got into it.*

A lot of my mates from school were in the same boat, so I decided to start a team myself. I rounded all of my Westcliff mates up, but we were still short of numbers, and that's when I decided to give Faisal 'Manjdog' Manji a call. Faisal was my best friend at primary school. His parents would work long hours just like mine, so we would go to the Late Stay after-school class where we'd do our homework and hang out. We had lost touch over the years, as he'd gone to the other grammar school, KEGS. Luckily, his team had just finished up too, and he was able to bring along five or six lads from KEGS with him to play. Things were starting to look promising.

However, getting a squad together was just one of the challenges that presented itself. I also had to secure our place in a league by proving that I was eligible and organised enough to run my own team at 16 years of age, which involved going to a meeting with the local FA. I put on my smartest clothes, polished my shoes and even put a comb through my hair. This was serious, after all. I was ushered into a dark room, where a load of old, grey men with notepads sat at a table staring at me very seriously. I remember thinking at the time that it was strange how a group of pensioners got to decide the fate of youth football teams, but that wasn't something I had any control over. I had to make a case for us being able to start this football team, so I cleared my throat, put on my most severe face and told them why they should let us join the league.

I walked out with the green light to start the team. I was buzzing. We still needed money, though. Even at youth level, running an amateur team can be an expensive business with costs such as kits, balls, pitch rental and referees. I was on a roll with officialdom, so I arranged another meeting, this time with the local council who were offering grants for new initiatives in the area. I had to convince the council that their money would be put to good use by helping us extend our amateur football careers.

'Look, we're all sixteen, and we just want to play football. You wouldn't want us milling about on the streets with nothing better to do now, would you?' Whether a bunch of grammar-school kids on the streets would strike fear into the heart of anyone was a moot point. But it worked. I got a £500 grant which went a long way to securing our new team's future.

I knew just the place to find a manager, too. My dad is a qualified sports injury therapist at pro level, and there's not much he doesn't know about the game. I asked him to be the gaffer, and he was delighted to do it. He kindly offered to sponsor the team which would also help to push his business. I told you he was an entrepreneur. He wanted to name the team after his company, Carmichael-Browns, but FA rules prohibited sponsoring youth teams, so we got round the rules by calling the team Carmichael-Browns Athletic. We could certainly justify giving the team our family name, even though everyone today thinks the team, which we called CBA for short, stood for something else: Can't Be A****.

Things felt like they really came together for me that summer. I got pretty good exam results after working harder than I ever had for my GCSEs, but football was the real catalyst.

We now had a team, and I was hanging out with a great bunch of lads. I was spending a lot of time with the boys from KEGS, as they lived closer to me than most of the Westcliff lads, and on the last day of summer before we all started sixth form we were mucking about in Chelmsford, having a laugh, when one of the boys said, 'Why don't you just come to KEGS?'

If only! Going to KEGS would have saved me an hour-long commute each way to school, and when I'd been unhappy in my first couple of years at Westcliff, with only Bob the bus driver to chat to, I'd applied each year to get in – and always just missed out. It was a tough school to get into at the best of times, let alone on the last day of summer with school starting the next day.

'Yeah, but what have you got to lose?' asked my friend. So I rang up KEGS, more as a bit of banter with the guys than anything else, and when a man I would later discover to be the deputy head answered the phone I said, 'Hello, I was wondering if I could come to your school, please.' I even said it in a comedy voice. I turned to my mates, laughing, expecting the line to go dead at any second.

To my amazement, he asked for my GCSE grades, and upon hearing them said, 'Yes, well, I think we can fit you in. Come to the induction day tomorrow and if you like it, you can start.'

If I'm being totally honest, after bunking off sick from the first day of Westcliff sixth form to attend the KEGS induction day, I still had no intention of going to KEGS. My main ambition was to use the day as a recruitment opportunity and tap up some more players for CBA. I told you I'd always wanted to run a football club! However, I had so much fun on the day and made so many new friends that I started to seriously contemplate it. That night, after crisis talks with Faisal, Seb, the Westcliff lads, my parents and anyone who would listen, I decided to call Westcliff and tell them I wasn't coming back. I was changing sixth-form school at ridiculously late notice.

Going to KEGS was a gamechanger for me. I'd settled eventually at Westcliff and made some good friends, but I would still see them playing football. KEGS meant that I got that time spent commuting to school back, which naturally meant more time to play football and football video games. I was the new boy once again, but I'd had plenty of practice at that by now, and besides, I had all my football mates to hang around with. Most importantly of all, KEGS had drama classes (Westcliff had disappointingly dropped drama from the curriculum when I was in Year 8) and something called the Fleur de Lys (FDL), which would give me the opportunity to show off my middle-child syndrome once again.

Everyone in sixth form wanted to be part of FDL, which was essentially a comedy club masquerading as a debating society. The FDL also did a lot of charity fundraising and hosted school assemblies every Friday morning. But Friday lunchtime was the main event – the debate. Only sixth-formers were allowed to attend and no one missed it: there'd be 150 adolescents packed into a classroom, a crazy atmosphere, to watch speeches by the committee members. I'd never seen anything like it.

Of course, I wanted to be a part of it, so I did my election speech – just as anyone who wanted to join it had to – which went well, and I was voted in by the committee. Once you were in the FDL it meant that you'd be one of the people delivering a speech on Fridays, in which you'd do your best to prove a certain point while taking the mick out of your fellow students and teachers, and I loved every minute of it. It certainly gave me a taste for getting up on a stage and performing in front of people, although sadly a year later, when the year below us took the helm, the FDL was shut down because someone uploaded a video of one of the speeches that went a bit too far onto YouTube and some parents took exception to it. Proof perhaps that not everything we do in life needs putting up on the internet.

While I was at KEGS I converted to the role of centre-back for CBA and we managed to win the league cup in our debut season. Leading my mates to a 3–0 win against Hannakins Farm at Witham Town's stadium was a real highlight for me, and at the time this was by far the best thing I'd achieved on a football pitch. Faisal Manji was on fire that year, racking up a total of nearly 40 goals and assists. After two years of Under-18s football, we capped it off with an overseas tour to Rimini in Italy, where we had a fantastic time. Everything about CBA was great fun.

I left KEGS in 2007 with my A levels and a place to do English Literature at Reading University, but it was the FDL that gave me my real education. University was a bit of a culture shock after sixth form, and in my second and third years I only had about three or four hours a week of seminars or face-to-face time with the teaching staff. I'd gone from a school where you had to work ridiculously hard in order to keep up with everyone in your class, to a place where the learning was essentially left up to you. Either do it or don't.

Most of my week was made up of 'reading' time, which basically meant I played football every day (by this time I'd improved enough to play for the university team, which was a pretty decent standard), hosted a university radio show with my room-mate Greg Osborne, and performed in stand-up gigs three times a week.

Telling jokes on stage was never going to stop for me just because I wasn't at school any more. The FDL had given me some great experience and allowed me to develop my skills and material, so I assumed I'd be well prepared for life on the comedy circuit.

As I drove down to Newbury for my first ever gig with Greg, however, I was no longer quite so certain. Greg was there for moral support – it's always good to have a friendly face in the crowd, unless there's hardly anyone in the crowd, of course. The gig was in a seedy bar and, unusually for a first-time performer in an industry where you can expect to do hundreds of gigs before you get paid for one, I was getting the outrageous sum of £100. In need of a comedy mentor prior to the gig, I'd turned to the collected wisdom of the internet, which had advised embellishing any experience I had in order to get a gig. I might have embellished a little too much …

Needless to say, it was terrible. I did a half-hour show, which is ludicrous for a first-time comic, and it was like a hen do in there – literally. The heckles came thick and fast from a load of middle-aged women smashed off their faces as I laboured through 28 minutes of awful jokes I'd written and about 2 minutes of better stuff I would use again. It would have been perfect for a 2-minute gig, and that was pretty much the material I based my show around after that. It would be another couple of years before I did another half-hour gig.

Most of my gigs were in London, and I would travel in to do anything from an open mic with three people in the crowd to later doing gigs with some really decent stand-ups, like Stephen Merchant and Kevin Bridges. Tom Rosenthal started around the same time I was doing it, and I was in the Reading Comedy Festival New Act Final with TV's Rob Beckett, who won. I've since teamed up with both Tom and Rob for various projects.

A typical gag of mine back then went something like this: 'My girlfriend talks a lot. I mean she really talks a lot. I call her Radio Three because I never listen to her.' That always got a good laugh – not that I actually had a girlfriend. My love life was the real joke then, but what I didn't realise was that I was building the foundations for something in the future. When my room in university halls sprung a leak one day, soaking a load of my stuff, I was fuming. I had to move rooms ... to an all-girls' floor. I couldn't believe my luck – and nor could my jealous mates. My next-door neighbour was a girl called Alex, and we quickly became friends. I obviously made a good impression because I managed to get her to agree to go out with me – three years later.

My 'Don't Stop Me Now' video-upload experience had done nothing to dim my taste for putting up videos of myself – it had only encouraged me. I would put up silly little comedy videos with characters I'd created and my live sets, with no real thought or game plan behind them. I was just having fun. I didn't really know if it would go anywhere and my football mates would give me some stick for being 'that YouTube guy', but the videos got me into a competition to be a T4 presenter on Channel 4. I got to the final stage of the process, but when I learned I would have to drop out of uni if I won, I dropped out of the competition instead.

The experience did give me one piece of broadcasting advice that I still use in every single video I make today. When I was doing the auditions for the show, one of the producers said to me, 'The trick to being a good TV presenter is to talk to the camera like it's your friend.' I took that advice literally, and that's why I start all of my videos with, 'Alright, mate, how you doing?' That's how I'd talk to a friend in real life, and that's the difference between YouTube and television: on YouTube you're watching a friend, not a celebrity or presenter.

Even without the T4 gig I would still make my television debut during university, though I definitely can't claim to be the first in my family to be on the telly. My mum is a TV game-show nut. Name a show, she's been on it: *The Crystal Maze, Wipeout, Pets Win Prizes, Supermarket Sweep, Surprise, Surprise*. She's crazy for them, so I should have sensed something was going on when she told me she had a spare ticket to watch Graham Norton's show *Totally Saturday* being filmed at the BBC in London.

What I didn't know at the time was that the premise of the show was for two unsuspecting members of the audience to be surprised, and they'd be joined by their families, who were hiding out backstage, to compete for a holiday. I was interested in TV production and I was about to do an internship with Channel 4 for a few months over the summer, so I was having a good look around from my seat in the audience, watching and learning, when I set my eyes upon the autocue and saw my own name on it. What on earth?

This was my big reveal coming up, but instead of looking surprised when the cameras settled on me, I was glaring at my mum going, 'I cannot believe you have stitched me up!'

Thankfully the audience saw the funny side when I said I'd seen it coming on the autocue.

My dad, brothers and two of my mates from football, Woody and Nash, came out from backstage and we competed against the other person who'd no doubt been stitched up too by someone in their family. It wasn't to be their day, though. My family are so competitive and up for anything that when we did the challenge we really went to town on the other family and destroyed them at the game. When I got the winning points I ran towards the crowd like Cristiano Ronaldo does when he scores a goal. 'Come on!' I screamed, flexing my much less impressive physique.

Graham Norton had one last surprise up his sleeve. 'Spencer, this isn't your first time being a little famous, is it?' he said. And then they played my 'Don't Stop Me Now' video on national television. Cheers, Graham.

# 3

## KOMPANY MAN

With Mum and Dad working so hard to provide for us when we were kids, we didn't have a lot of time for family holidays. So it made perfect sense that, having won one together as a family on *Totally Saturday*, we'd each go on separate holidays!

I went out to America for a dream post-university trip with Woody and Nash to Los Angeles and San Diego, California. It was a cool holiday, even if the cosmetic smiles and fake boobs of LA weren't exactly my cup of tea. I knew after two weeks that going travelling for any length of time (like a lot of my friends were) just wasn't for me. I was already getting restless and desperate to get on with my life.

I came back without much of a clue about what exactly it was I wanted to do. Given that I'd enjoyed doing radio and stand-up so much, and with no other ideas immediately presenting themselves to me, I thought I'd give the comedy game more of a crack. The Edinburgh Festival seemed like a good option to scope out the very best talent and do a few shows myself, maybe even get noticed by an agent. And when a fellow aspiring stand-up I met told me he had some accommodation up there and I could stay with him, it seemed like things were falling neatly into place.

Maybe a little too neatly. As soon as we got up there, it became clear that I had been a bit quick to trust the word of this guy. His name was Bob and it turned out there was no accommodation (and no chance of getting any, given how busy Edinburgh gets at festival time), and to top it off he was skint. He was hoping I'd be paying his way too! Stitched up was the expression that came immediately to mind.

Still, we were there now, so we had to make the best of it – and we ended up loving it. Bob turned out to be a really good lad and a lot of fun despite his organisational missteps. We watched some amazing stand-ups, who were just incredible to see, and then from about two until six in the morning I'd turn up at open-mic gigs and try to get a five-minute set. After that we'd head off for three or four hours' sleep, only to do it all again the next day.

On the first night it was raining, which immediately put restrictions on sleeping rough, so we climbed the fence in a park and slept under an ice-cream van. I was grateful that I'd remembered to bring Saunders's army-cadet sleeping bag with me, though it was still pretty grim having a four-wheeled rather than four-poster bed. On the second night we managed to get into a block of flats – some people might call this 'breaking and entering', but it was a victimless crime, honest (we didn't even break anything) – and slept rough in the corridor, and on the third night we just stayed up all night and got the train home first thing. It was a great experience and I got plenty of stage-time in, but the agents weren't exactly queuing up outside the front door of wherever I was sleeping that night.

To make it in stand-up you've got to be committed, and you might be plugging away for up to ten years before you make any kind of success of it – if at all. And there's no doubt that this was starting to play on my mind. When a gig went well and everything worked, I loved it, but I hated the gigs that didn't. Don't get me wrong, by the end I was doing well most nights that I performed, but I had a bit of a realisation during a gig up at Lincoln University Student Union that maybe it wasn't for me any more.

Student Unions tended to be my best crowds, especially given that I was fresh out of university myself at the time and could relate to the audience well. There were about 150 students there for the gig, and I was getting paid something like £100. Once you'd factored in petrol and everything else it was more like £50.

Before I set off, I uploaded one of my comedy videos onto YouTube. Eight hours later, I arrived back at home shattered, with the post-gig high having worn off long ago in the car. I put my computer on and saw it straight away: my video had over 2,000 views. I'd just spent eight hours earning £50 and performing in front of 150 people, when my video in that time had been seen by thousands.

Something clicked for me then. I'm an efficient guy, as I've said, and these were numbers that added up to me. I would go up to Edinburgh the following year with Alex, just as a punter. Pitching the idea of sleeping rough under an ice-cream van to her would have been tough, and thankfully I had enough money and foresight this time to actually book some hotels. The standard at Edinburgh is so, so high, and I'd only ever been average, if I'm honest. We had a great time just watching the best at work.

The online videos, on the other hand, I could see a future in them. I'd done internships at Channel 4 during university, and had learned a lot and got to do some pretty cool things like shadowing Derren Brown for a week (with his permission, of course – I wasn't just following him on the sly). Channel 4 had offered me a job in their corporate-relations department, which I turned down. Doing something corporate just wasn't for me. But when I learned that a mate, Ross, from the year above at Westcliff school had started working for a small production company called BigBalls, I thought, *This is more like it*.

I bombarded him with messages, saying things like, 'Mate, I made this YouTube video. I'll come in and work for you guys for free.' I didn't let up for a second and Ross, who is a good lad, was a little slow to send my videos on for my liking, probably because he was still focusing on making a good impression himself. So I decided to take action more fitting for a company called BigBalls. I went on their website and sent an email to everyone whose email address I could find saying:

Hi guys,

My name's Spencer. I'm Ross's mate. I know he's mentioned me already because he told me he has. He loves my YouTube videos, so do a small but growing amount of people online. Some of my videos are good, some are rubbish – here they are for you to have a look at. Let me come and work for you for free.

Spence

I wasn't actually sure whether or not he'd sent my videos on, so in a way I may have been stitching Ross up (if you're reading this, sorry, mate), but no harm was done and if you want something badly enough, sometimes you've just got to reach out and grab it. And it worked for me: a guy called Rich at the company really liked one of the videos I'd done.

I'd made a mock advertisement for the soft drink Mountain Dew, full of silly little slogans, and Mountain Dew had shared it on their Facebook page. It got a load of likes on Facebook, and this was at a time when I left all my email alerts active on my YouTube channel, so every time someone liked a video or subscribed I'd get an email telling me. I'd been out playing football that day, and when I came home I had over a thousand emails in my inbox!

Even though I hadn't made it for Mountain Dew, and indeed some of it was taking the mick out of their product, they'd had a good enough sense of humour about it to share it. BigBalls focused mostly on making advertising content for brands, so Rich said, 'This is our cup of tea – an irreverent video with a bit of comedy for a brand. Look, we're a small company and we don't have anything for you, but we do have a sister company who are making this football video game. Do you like video games?'

Did I like video games? More specifically, did I like football video games? I totally lucked out, as the sister company We R Interactive were making a brand-new football game on Facebook, a first-person game intertwined with real-life footage called *I Am Playr*, and at 21 years of age I became the community manager for the game, looking after their social media – a proper, salary-paying job.

The game was way ahead of its time. It incorporated things like the kind of girls you liked (a footballer's essential, obviously) and the path your playing career took, as well as gameplay. It was basically a very early version of 'The Journey' mode you can now find on *FIFA*. It was very slick, and professional footballers like Lee Dixon and Steven Gerrard were involved in it. I met up with these guys to do interviews and make content with them, and it was great rubbing shoulders with some of the top players in the country and doing a bit of presenting.

I had a good thing going, making YouTube videos at home in the evening and doing a job that was perfectly suited to me in the day. I really liked that job and the people I worked with, but the minute I stopped feeling it, I quit.

I've always had something in me that makes me think I'm never going to do something I don't want to do. I decided pretty early on that my most valuable currency was time, not money, and so I was always willing to do loads of things for free. Don't get me wrong, money is very useful, but I always believed that once I'd found what I wanted to do I'd work hard to get really good at it, and then money would come along with it. But I'd never do something I didn't want to do, and I'd reached that point with doing tweets and managing a Facebook page for someone else. There was no grey area for me; it was all black or white. My passion for things like

YouTube had grown and I wanted to make my own content, so that was it for me: I was leaving. Though history would have to repeat itself before I finally got around to making my own stuff for real.

After I quit I spent the summer of 2011 presenting the live version of the TV game show *Minute to Win It* – one of the few my mum hadn't appeared on – which was presented by Joe Swash and Caroline Flack. I basically did the shows on the road where they didn't have the budget to pay Joe Swash. If I learned one thing that summer it was that I'm not the best at faking enthusiasm. If I'm naturally into something then great, I'm super-pumped: Let's go! That's why I love doing my own stuff. But I found it harder to do something I didn't really believe in.

I distinctly remember being shouted at through my ear-piece by the director in the middle of a live show to 'look like you want to be here'. The truth was, I didn't. Well, not for ever, anyway. It was good fun for a few months, but pretty soon I wanted to do something different again.

My dad gave me a job at his new renewable energy company that he ran with my brother Seb for a while, and a lot of my mates would say, 'What are you doing? A minute ago you were interviewing Steven Gerrard, now you're driving a Transit van delivering solar panels!' I could feel the clock ticking a bit, and still living at home was hardly living the dream. But then a job working for a very different kind of Kompany came my way.

I got a phone call from BigBalls saying that Vincent Kompany, the Manchester City and Belgium captain, had been in touch because he was looking for a social-media guy, and they thought I could be it. Sure, I might have quit my last job because I'd had enough of doing social media for someone else, but this was the sickest version of that job: good money for not even full-time hours and a seat in Vincent's box for every home game at the Etihad.

'Yeah,' I said, immediately putting my principles to one side in the glare of a job offer from one of the best players on the planet. 'I'll do it.'

So I went through the interview process, starting with meeting his people, which went well, and then I had to meet Vincent himself. We were originally going to meet after a game in London, but his schedule changed at the last minute so instead we did it over Skype. It won't surprise you to learn that I had no problem at all talking to him over an online camera, but for some reason my camera wasn't working on this occasion so all we had was audio.

Vincent was clearly a very switched-on businessman as well as a great player, and I told him about all the exciting things I thought we could do to give him a real social-media presence. I told him how much I looked up to him, how I was a defender too and in the end I just came out with, 'Come on, let's do this.'

'Yeah, cool,' he said. 'I just need to look you in the eye and make sure I can trust you.'

We quit the call. I got the camera working again and then called him back. His face was on the screen, totally impassive, just looking at me. It could only have been for a second, but I don't think I'd ever felt so self-conscious in my life, just sitting there, letting him judge what I looked like. And then, very coolly, he just said, 'Yeah, you're good.'

And that was that. I was now working for Vincent Kompany.

Immediately, it meant I could move out of my parents' house and head for the bright lights of London. I moved in with some mates in Angel, Islington, and I would go up to Manchester a couple of times a month, where I'd often go to stay at Vincent's house, and I even visited Patrick Vieira's house too. And the opportunities for name-dropping the best footballers around didn't stop there.

I got to hang out with Carlos Tévez, which for this West Ham fan was pretty cool given that he'd scored the goal that kept the club in the Premier League in 2007. The language barrier meant that the conversation wasn't exactly enthralling, but that hardly mattered when I went home to tell my jealous mates about it!

I would meet all the other City players too, going into the players' lounge after games, chatting to people like Yaya Touré and Sergio Agüero. One day, after a meeting at the club's training ground, Vincent was driving his Porsche on the motorway, with me in the passenger seat, when I looked across at the next car – another Porsche, naturally – and there was Mario Balotelli driving, giving us the eyes. He gave us a look that said, 'Uh-huh,' and Vincent gave him a look back, with his all-business face on … then Balotelli broke into a big grin and accelerated. Vincent followed suit, and we were zooming down the motorway[1]. It was crazy!

I was living the dream. The job at We R Interactive had been cool, but now I was properly in the football world. I was thrown in at the deep end, working closely with Manchester City, directing Q&As and productions in their ground well above my experience level. But the best part of the job was getting to know Vincent.

I think he was the best centre-back in the world that year – remember, this was *that* season, the 2011–12 season – and we got on really well. He's only a little bit older than me, and we'd speak on the phone about social-media ideas for ages and then just chat for half an hour like mates at the end. I couldn't believe it: I was 23 years old and friends with the Manchester City and Belgium captain.

[1]   All within the confines of the law, officer!

I've been lucky enough to meet and get to know a number of professional footballers in my career so far, and every now and then you meet one that really impresses you. When a footballer is a great talker, has a really amiable personality or just that little something special about him or her, people will often say that they are destined for a career on TV after hanging up their boots. Vincent, for me, was a step above the rest. He was intelligent, determined and diplomatic in a way that made him stand out from the crowd. Forget TV, I could see Vincent being the Prime Minister of Belgium when he finishes pocketing strikers for a living.

One final aspect of the job would have been the icing on the cake for some. I was getting paid really well to work four days a week, but in reality I could get most of the job done in six or seven hours if I worked hard, which left me plenty of free time to do things like go to the gym every day, play football and, of course, play *Football Manager*.

I started making YouTube videos regularly for the first time, instead of just putting them up every so often, and I finally turned my efforts away from the comedy videos I'd been doing and towards football content. Making football-related content was a really big step for me. Even though I'd been schooled in the encyclopaedia of football otherwise known as *Football Manager*, had improved hugely as a player to be able to play to a (semi-) decent standard and knew as much about football as anyone at the table, I still had a kid's mentality about being able to express my opinions to the world. I still felt like a little boy coming to the game late, so if I was faced with someone else who'd been kicking a ball since he was a toddler, I somehow felt a bit inferior and that I wasn't allowed to speak up. I thought that if I broadcast my thoughts to the world, there'd be someone in the comments saying, 'Yeah, but you weren't even in the football team till you were 14.'

Spending time with Vincent, arguing my point about players and backing myself when needed, had helped me shed some of this, but the biggest enabler to finally shed this mentality came from doing stand-up comedy. When doing a comedy gig, you can get up in front of a room full of people you don't know and say to yourself, 'What if they don't laugh?' Or you can say, 'None of these people know me. If something goes badly, they won't remember me tomorrow. The only person who will remember it was a bad gig is me, and if I choose to learn from it instead of fixate on it then it's a positive rather than a negative.' Just like playing *FIFA 98* with the mouse, I would either have a good gig or I'd learn.

You can take this mentality into anything. I applied it to approaching girls (before I got together with Alex, of course). If you approach a girl you like nicely and she's rude to you, you can choose to forget she exists straight after. There's a polite way to reject someone, and if she doesn't choose this option then she probably isn't worth it anyway. It doesn't have to affect your life. I took this attitude into my YouTube football videos, refusing to worry any more about whether anyone would react negatively to them or call me out as some kind of fraud – which in reality would never happen because no one but me cared that I got into football late.

Vincent didn't care about any of these extra-curricular activities – he just wanted the job done to a high standard and anything outside of that didn't matter to him. He was astute enough to know that, as he obviously earned an unbelievable amount of money, he could hardly be tight with paying his staff, so he was always very generous and looked after those who worked for him. I really respected him for that, and it's a lesson I certainly took from him.

I probably should have thought, *I've lucked out here*. But instead it had the opposite effect on me. It didn't sit well with me earning a really good wage and having all this free time. I started thinking it wasn't right, and if I wasn't being made to work hard in what I was doing I needed to find something else. Unbelievably, as we approached the business end of the 2011–12 football season, I was getting itchy feet once again.

I wanted to see the season out, as I'd only been working for Vincent for about seven months and he had been very good to me, so I canvassed the opinions of my dad, my brothers and loads of my mates. They all told me the same thing: 'Do not leave. Give it another year. You're young and there's no rush.'

Their advice was no doubt absolutely sound and logical, and whenever I run a vote on my YouTube channel now I always try to go with the majority – the people have spoken and all that. But on this occasion it took only one person to confirm what I already knew I should do. My friend Sam Rowland, who's a talented film director, was the lone voice of dissent. He simply said, 'Mate, if you don't want to be there you should leave.'

So I had this difficult discussion with Vincent at a time when he was captaining a team challenging for the title, playing must-win game after must-win game, and had much bigger things to worry about than the future of his social-media manager. I told his manager, a lovely guy called Klaas, that my heart wasn't in it and that it would make a dream job for someone else – just not me. Klaas invited me up to Manchester for what I assumed would be the courtesy of telling Vincent face to face.

Vincent and Klaas had other ideas. They had a league title to think about and just wanted to nip it in the bud. Over some food they asked, 'What can we do to keep you? Is it money?'

It definitely wasn't money, but it was difficult for them to understand why I would leave such a great job with nothing lined up to do instead. A better job would have made sense to them. I wanted to make more football YouTube videos, something I could easily have done on their watch as I had plenty of spare time, but it just didn't feel right. I knew I had to strike out on my own: I needed to give myself the fear.[2]

They offered me all sorts of incentives to keep me, all of which seemed great but I knew I had to stick to my guns, before Vincent offered to drive me to the station to head home. It was just me and Vincent in the car, and when he pulled up outside the train station he turned to me and said, 'Look, we've said what we want to say today. I think we've made our point, and it's up to you ultimately. But let me give you some advice, not as your boss, not as a footballer, but as a guy who's only a little bit older than you. I know you're an ambitious guy, and I respect that. If you stay for one more year you will leave with my utmost respect. I will be a guy you can always count on. Think about it.'

That was the first time I wavered throughout the whole process. It was only one more year, after all. I talked to Seb,

---

[2] 'The fear' was something I learned from the wise sages of the sitcom *Friends*, Joey Tribbiani and Chandler Bing. (Check out season 3, episode 10.) 'As long as you've got this job,' Joey explains to Rachel Green, whose fashion-industry dreams are floundering in a coffee-shop, 'you've got nothing pushing you to get another. You need the fear!'

who has always been the person I go to for advice when it comes to my career. His thoughts were unequivocal: 'Now you really have to stay!'

But when I thought about it, I knew I was going against that thing in me that says if I don't want to do something, I should stop doing it. As crazy as it sounded, I knew Vincent deserved better, and I couldn't carry on doing that job. I gave Vincent my decision and he wanted me to call it a day immediately. I left a couple of weeks before the end of the season.

On the final day of the football season in 2012 I was wearing a Manchester City shirt (which I justified to myself because West Ham were in the Championship that year). Like millions of fans around the world, I leapt to my feet as that amazing 'Agüero!' moment happened, when Sergio Agüero scored an injury-time winner to give Manchester City their first league title since the 1960s, winning it on goal difference in one of the most exciting season climaxes ever.

My first thought was purely, *Unbelievable! What a moment!*

I was over the moon for Vincent and the club.

My second thought was a bit less generous: *If only I'd stayed, I might have got a decent bonus!*

• • •

Only a week or so later I put up my first Premier League poem video on YouTube. It was hardly a Shakespearean-worthy piece of verse, but it was a fun, irreverent review of the season in a basic poem, and I was pretty proud of it. The amount of time I put into writing it and getting the footage together meant that I never would have made it if I'd still been working for Vincent. I'd have just gone to the gym or played *Football Manager* instead. I needed to give myself the fear, to have no job or money coming in to motivate me to get on and do it, and as soon as I put it up I knew right then that I'd made the correct decision.

My Premier League poem was my first big football video on YouTube. It got over 75,000 views on it in one day (a record for me) and that feeling was a bit of an 'Agüero!' moment for me personally – something money simply couldn't buy.

## 4

# BEHIND THE MASK: FIFA PLAYA

I didn't remain a free agent for long. BigBalls – who had hooked me up with the We R Interactive job and the Kompany role – got in touch once again and asked if I'd like to come and work for them, this time on a YouTube football channel. How could I turn that down?

BigBalls had won the pitch to make a YouTube Originals channel called Copa90, and I started work there about a month after leaving Vincent Kompany. I was only the second person employed to work on the channel, and I helped shape the identity of Copa90 and got some great presenters in. I produced a show called *EuroFan*, presented by DJ and comedian Tom Deacon, whose success in the Chortle Student Comedy competition was one of the inspirations for me doing stand-up in the first place.

My years of experience of doing my own material on YouTube helped massively, as I was able to bring strategic elements to putting our content up, such as when was the best time to do it to get the most views? What kind of videos should we be making? Who do we need to collaborate with?

Our goal, set by Google for that first year, was to get to 100,000 subscribers. Without hitting that target, we'd have to look elsewhere for future funding and we were starting from zero. No one knew who we were, so it was always going to be a challenge, and about eight months in we were off-target and it didn't look like we were going to make it. We did two major things to change that.

The first was approaching KSI, who is the UK's biggest YouTuber and a huge *FIFA* gamer, and asking him to do a show for us. Collaboration is the key to growing on YouTube: you can benefit from your collaborator sharing your content with their subscribers and vice versa. Although in this instance, given that we didn't have much to offer in the subscriber department, KSI had to make do with getting paid instead.

Being super-busy, KSI was impossible to get hold of, so in the end it was his newly appointed manager Liam who we chatted with. KSI agreed to present a show for us, where he would go to various Champions League football matches around Europe, and share it with his subscribers and tell them to check out Copa90. I produced the show, which is how I got to know KSI, and I consider him to be a good friend now. That's the other bonus with collaborating – you get to meet some great new people.

It turned out to be money well spent, as KSI helped us gain loads of new subscribers, but despite his incredible influence, it looked like we were still going to fall short of that magic number of 100,000. We had other obligations on the channel too, like making a certain amount of original content, and we were running out of money, so we couldn't just continue paying YouTubers to front videos and help us hit the number. We needed to make more affordable content that would still be effective in bringing in more subscribers. It didn't seem like an easy problem to solve.

I thought to myself, *Why is KSI so successful?* And the thing I kept coming back to, apart from his larger-than-life personality, was his *FIFA* content. At this point in early 2013, the YouTube *FIFA* community was growing rapidly thanks to popular game-modes such as Ultimate Team. Why couldn't we make our own *FIFA* content too? It was cheap, easy to produce and I absolutely loved *FIFA*, so we were well stocked in the passion department. I'd never made a single gaming video in my life before this point, but it now seemed clear to me that our own *FIFA* show was exactly what we needed to push us over the edge.

So, along with another guy who worked at Copa90 called Neil Smythe, we came up with the idea for someone to play a comedy character on the show with a hidden identity – like the Stig on *Top Gear* – and he would play *FIFA* against celebrities and other YouTubers. Collaboration, as ever, was key, and these other YouTubers could ask people to check out our content on Copa90 and, if they liked it, subscribe. At this stage we didn't know who would play the character, but we thought we had a fairly foolproof plan to get the subscribers we needed.

Some of my colleagues weren't quite so convinced by it, however. I arrived at one meeting to find that our *FIFA* show had been wiped from the programmes-in-development board, and I couldn't believe it. I was convinced that the channel would be sunk without its own *FIFA* show, and if we didn't make it to 100,000 subscribers, we could all lose our jobs.

I was so convinced, in fact, that in a meeting when I was making my point – probably a little too forcefully, as I was known to do at the time, but that's just my enthusiasm getting the better of me – I put my own job on the line if the *FIFA* show didn't get us enough new subscribers. Andrew Conrad, a very experienced TV producer who called the shots, was willing to back me; however, he was equally willing to say, 'If it doesn't work out, Spence, you're going to lose your job.'

Fine. If we didn't make it to 100,000 subscribers we could all be out of our jobs anyway. The show was a goer – and maybe I needed the fear once again to really make it work.

The first thing we needed to sort was who would play our masked *FIFA* player. It had to be someone pretty decent at *FIFA* so we could at least make it competitive with some of the other *FIFA* YouTubers. He needed to be pretty funny too, so that he could be cocky enough to play this delusional character who thinks he's the best at *FIFA*.

The show would work so that when our *FIFA* player won, it would make for quite a big thing, this mystery man beating a seasoned YouTuber with half a million subscribers who would have to do some kind of *FIFA* apology if they lost.[3] So whoever played him would need a pretty thick skin. But if our *FIFA* player lost, he'd have to do a much more embarrassing forfeit.

We started casting, and we couldn't find anyone. The only person who showed any promise at all was David Vujanic, who already presented a show called *Comments Below* for the channel. The problem was that he was six-foot-five tall, so you'd be able to work out who was behind the mask straight

[3] A *FIFA* apology is where the loser will publicly acknowledge the superiority of the winner and apologise for their performance. Depending on the manner and margin of defeat they can range from the mildly embarrassing to the completely demeaning, with all kinds of shades of grey in between.

away. We needed someone a little less conspicuous if we were to maintain his secret identity as a talking point. And then someone said, 'Spence, why don't you do it?'

Now, it would be stretching credulity just a little to suggest that the idea hadn't crossed my mind, but because I had championed the show so passionately, I hadn't wanted people to think it was just because I wanted to be the star of it. But if someone else suggested it, well, how could I refuse? 'OK, then,' I said, with just the right amount of reluctance in my voice, 'I'll do it.'

We still hadn't worked out exactly what the character I'd play would be, and we did a pilot show with the character called the *FIFA* Gimp, with me dressed in an orange morph suit with eye holes cut out so I could see the screen. It was every bit as terrible as that sentence suggests. In fact, it was worse – and what made it worse still was that the first big YouTubers for the show were already booked in for the following week.

With the clock ticking, I came up with the name FIFA Playa the day before we made the trailer. He was a wannabe gangsta, a gamer from the streets, but really he was just a geek in a mask. We needed to sort his look out pronto, so naturally we headed down to the home of quality costume design, Sports Direct, where we picked up a Lonsdale cap and a snood. I summoned the spirit of Ali G and perfected my best mock 'urban' accent (which in reality sounded like a poor imitation of radio's Tim Westwood). We were ready. Or at least more ready.

We put the trailer out with the FIFA Playa in fine obnoxious form, burning £5 notes as if to say, 'I don't need the money, mate.' The FIFA Playa's message to his opponents was simple: 'If you lose, you're going to get mugged off in front of the whole of YouTube.' The trailer went viral – thankfully without the need for me to get my top off and sing 'Don't Stop Me Now' – and the general reaction seemed to be, 'Who the hell is this guy?'

Fifa Playa made his debut against NepentheZ in February 2013, talking the talk but failing to deliver on the pitch, going down on penalties. His punishment? A relatively tame one compared to the standards of later episodes, but it still involved standing in the middle of a rush-hour tube carriage in London and announcing an apology to NepentheZ at the top of his voice – something I'd not be too keen on doing as myself. But, as Batman no doubt agrees, it's amazing the power of a mask.

The FIFA Playa would play a different YouTuber every week, and it proved a huge hit with the viewers, as we easily reached and then surpassed our subscriber target. We were all going to keep our jobs. Phew! I couldn't have been happier for our channel, and I didn't really have time to feel vindicated or anything like that – I was having too much fun doing the show.

In an early episode the Playa took on KSI's brother ComedyShortsGamer. We headed over to a nice little corner of Hertfordshire where the two brothers lived together with their parents, and I waited outside in full FIFA Playa clobber while the production team got things set up in the living room.

Now, I hadn't quite appreciated just how dodgy I looked in my snood and hoodie, lurking outside the respectable home of a couple of YouTube superstars, but then the curtains started twitching and I could see people looking out at me. Finally, a neighbour's front door opened and a woman shouted at me, 'What are you doing here? We've called the police so you'd better clear off.'

Steady on! My voice slipped back out from the ghetto into the friendlier land of Essex grammar-school boy and I pulled my mask down and said, 'It's all fine – we're just filming something. Please don't send the police! I'm nice really.'

Once inside the KSI–ComedyShortsGamer household, however, the snood remained firmly in place. I knew KSI well from producing his Copa90 *Road to Wembley* show, but he had no idea who the FIFA Playa was, and I intended to keep it that way. I remained 'in character' for the entire time, even when the camera wasn't rolling, to maintain the mystery. It was the worst kind of method acting for everyone in the vicinity as the FIFA Playa was such an obnoxious individual. To make things worse for ComedyShortsGamer, I beat him in our match, and he delivered what was surely a heartfelt apology to the camera by way of punishment.

We knew that keeping the FIFA Playa identity a secret was vital to the show's appeal, and the speculation over who he really was only helped the buzz around it. There were times when the mask was a hindrance, however – and not just on KSI's street.

When the FIFA Playa went to the FIFA Interactive World Cup to play two-time world champion Alfonso Ramos, we warned the event organisers in advance that I'd be arriving as a masked character. We included some photos of what I'd look like and told them to be prepared, because they wouldn't be used to having someone like the FIFA Playa in the press box.

'No problem,' they said.

When we turned up, however, they wouldn't let us in. 'Guys, we talked about this,' I said. 'It's not really a wannabe gangsta here to cause mayhem in the competition. It's a character, and you invited us to come in the first place.'

No dice. We had to film the piece with Alfonso after hours instead, and it was as FIFA Playa that I beat the two-time world champion. The shirt I mentioned earlier actually reads, 'To the FIFA Playa, you're the best FIFA Player in the world.'

We upped the stakes with the punishments and apologies in the show in some surreal ways. I put dog food all over my face and had CapgunTom's dog lick it off. When I lost to RossiHD, who lived in the south-west of England, the home of graffiti artist Banksy, I had to spray-paint how bad I was at *FIFA* all over a wall. (Don't try this at home, kids.)

We flew out to Reykjavik to play GudjonDaniel and he beat me, so my punishment was to go to the middle of a shopping centre and admit to the world I'd been taught a *FIFA* lesson by Iceland's 'national hero'. If you'd told me a year before I'd be sitting in a motorised children's car in an Icelandic shopping centre saying, 'I am a chav,' to camera, I would have thought I'd had some kind of mental breakdown.

• • •

As we developed the character the FIFA Playa's aggressive 'urban' accent was soon ancient history, replaced by more of a raspy mockney tone. We wanted to make the character more self-deprecating and likeable than the earlier version. Whatever accent he sported, there was plenty of ridiculous rhetoric to keep everyone entertained and appalled in equal measure. He'd remind everyone of his vibrant background by opening the show with his rap alias and one of his gangster nicknames:

'Yo, what's up. It's your boy the FIFA Playa, aka Lethal Injection, aka Stevie Two Shoes.'

FIFA Playa was raised on the streets by a Belgian lady called Marie, but he maintained that his biological father was a guy called Edgar Allen Sports (EA Sports). He had some serious daddy issues, as he believed his father had invented the game (when in fact it was the company EA Sports) and that was why he was so good at it. Reality would bite soon enough for the FIFA Playa.

All the *FIFA* roads on YouTube seemed to point towards its biggest star, and while FIFA Playa had won and lost against some of the most well-known and talented players in the world, he could not escape his destiny. He had to face KSI in the match to end all matches.

The build-up was huge, with YouTubers like Dirty Mike, AirJapes, R9Rai and MGH throwing their opinions around as to who would come out on top, the majority of them tipping KSI, which did not sit well with the so-called son of Edgar Allen Sports.

By this time KSI was starting to suspect the FIFA Playa's secret identity. It probably wasn't that hard, given that we'd been spending a lot of time together with me producing his show, and when word got out that he was saying he thought I was the FIFA Playa, we knew it was time to take action and throw him off the scent.

One day, when we were doing some filming for his show in Trafalgar Square, we had someone from the office of similar height and build to me, a lad called Tom Pryce, dress up as the FIFA Playa. He turned up in the middle of the shoot and didn't say a word – he just photobombed it and ran off. KSI stood there saying, 'What the … ?' while we all looked on. Now that he had seen FIFA Playa and me in the same place, he couldn't possibly continue to think it was me, could he?

He wasn't the only one who got suspicious. One particularly dedicated YouTuber managed to find some videos from my own channel (which wasn't very big at the time so must have taken some finding – I was just a guy working behind the camera at Copa90) and used them in a video he made comparing the freckles on my arm in one of my personal videos with those on the arms of the FIFA Playa, coming to the conclusion that it must be me. This level of forensic detail was starting to get a bit *CSI* for me, though it only added to the appeal of the show.

In the build-up to the showdown with KSI, the FIFA Playa assumed the lotus position on a tyre swing on a housing estate; he pumped some serious iron, and announced to the world: 'It's the battle of the big dogs. Lucky for him, I'm wearing a muzzle!'

KSI was no less determined, giving plenty back: 'You've been tormenting me all these months. So many people constantly asking, "Who is this FIFA Playa?" Well, I'm here. Come on, are you scared or something?'

The stage was set, and KSI's living room wouldn't suffice for a major head-to-head like this, especially if his neighbours didn't like the look of a snood-wearing prowler once again. Instead, the Playa and KSI took their positions in a boxing ring in the Lonsdale boxing club, gloving up and walking out dramatically with their respective ringside allies in tow – the #PlayaArmy and KSI's mates.

One of KSI's cornermen was none other than Simon Minter, aka MiniMinter, someone who has gone on to absolutely smash YouTube and be a huge part of KSI's group the Sidemen. And if you look in my corner, two of the lads behind the Playa Army masks were actually my brothers Seb and Saunders, proof that they've been supporting me since day one, only here they were doing it under their Playa Army aliases Macca and Lil Fif.

KSI and FIFA Playa did the obligatory eyeball-to-eyeball stare-down at one another, and took their positions in the ring, mano a mano. And then we took our boxing gloves off to play, obviously. It wouldn't have made for much of a match with them on.

The stakes were high: KSI would have to concede his position as the number-one *FIFA* YouTuber and admit that the FIFA Playa was top dog if he lost; while something unspeakable would be done to FIFA Playa in the Ultimate Fighting cage if he tasted defeat. And there was the literally small matter of the tiny trophy inscribed with KING OF FIFA up for grabs too.

FIFA Playa took charge of Real Madrid while KSI had Bayern Munich at his command, and KSI won a tight match 1–0, the first of a best of three. The second time around the Playa's Swansea side were against KSI's Northampton team (with Adebayo 'The Beast' Akinfenwa leading the line), and the Playa didn't disappoint this time, winning the match with a goal in the last-minute of extra time, sending the Playa Army – all six of them – wild in trademark machine-gun celebration. At one match each, there had to be a decider.

An emotional connection informed the team picks this time. KSI chose the team he supports, Arsenal, and FIFA chose Brazil, the country of his birth, or so he claimed. KSI took the lead and tore around the ring, finishing with an elbow drop to the mat in, frankly, an over-the-top moment of celebration. It wouldn't last, however, and when the land of the nuts levelled the score, it was time for a well-rehearsed hand-grenade celebration with the Playa Army.

Over the course of three matches there was still nothing to choose between the FIFA Playa and KSI, so extra time and then potentially penalties would be required to separate them. KSI isn't the number-one YouTuber for nothing, though, and he still had a little something left in the locker. With penalties looming, he managed to steal a winner – celebrating this time with an off-the-rope high-five with his corner. He then closed out the match. It was the ultimate #MiseryCompiler for Stevie Steak Knife.

Nothing, however, could have prepared the FIFA Playa for the true brutality that was to follow from KSI's mouth. 'You do know that EA Sports isn't a person,' he said. 'It's a company.' The quick check on Wikipedia that followed was enough to guarantee that this was the biggest fatherly revelation on camera since Luke Skywalker found out about his parentage at the end of *Star Wars: The Empire Strikes Back*.

There was the small matter of the punishment to come too, in which the FIFA Playa was padded up and KSI put his gloves back on. 'You don't know how many people would love this opportunity,' the FIFA Playa said in a rare moment of insight. KSI then went to town on the Playa, in some very family-unfriendly moments of violence, which have now been witnessed by millions of people online.

● ● ●

FIFA Playa's revelation allowed us to make a mockumentary series that had less to do with him challenging other YouTubers and more to do with his life. *Behind the Mask* saw

FIFA Playa get fired from Copa90 and then do pretty much everything he could to get himself a second series.

*Behind the Mask* was one of the most creatively rewarding projects I've had the pleasure to work on, and it was a testament to everyone at Copa90's hard work that we'd been able to take a character based around a video game and make a whole series about him without a minute of *FIFA* action in it. Lawrence Tallis in particular deserves a lot of credit in helping form the character of FIFA Playa – it definitely wasn't a one-man effort.

The *Behind the Mask* story included all kinds of escapades, with the Playa getting his bum out in public, smashing up Sean Wright-Phillips at *FIFA* like a Greek plate and coming face to face with his lunatic superfan Thomas Gray. It wouldn't be the last time he ran into him. When he had a crystal-ball-based epiphany up in Edinburgh during the comedy festival (no ice-cream van included this time), the Playa knew what he must do next: *Xtreme FIFA*.

Simply playing the game against other YouTubers had, in the Playa's own words, become 'too easy'. *Xtreme FIFA* would change all that, as it would now involve playing in extreme conditions to make things more interesting. The show even came with a warning:

WARNING: The people in this video are trained FIFA professionals. For your own safety, do not attempt to play FIFA in the conditions you are about to see.

The first episode saw the Playa take on an old foe, GudjonDaniel of Iceland. To put the extreme into the challenge, they'd be playing in sub-zero conditions in the Ice Bar in London. To make things truly Xtreme, however, they had to shed an item of clothing if they failed to score within various timeframes, and each time one of them conceded a goal, they had to eat an ice cube. Brrrr! Down to their T-shirts in the freezing cold, the Playa had his revenge on 'chicken' GudjonDaniel and made it clear that, when things got Xtreme, the Playa got Xtremer.

Things got even more extreme soon after when the Playa faced the world's strongest footballer, Adebayo 'The Beast' Akinfenwa, a proper *FIFA* legend and someone who has gone on to become a true friend of mine. In the words of the Playa: 'He's the strongest player in *FIFA*, and I'm the strongest at *FIFA*.' Fittingly for a specimen like Akinfenwa, the game was played in a gym and each player took turns to do a physical challenge like bench-pressing or doing arm curls at the blow of a whistle while his controller lay idle.

Akinfenwa was a great sport, and he smashed the physical challenges, of course. We had some other great footballers on, too, who really got into the spirit of it. KSI and the FIFA Playa went round to Arsenal left-back Kieran Gibbs's house to do a two vs two match, along with Wojciech Szczęsny, who was Arsenal's keeper at the time, on KSI's channel and then

*Xtreme FIFA.* We blindfolded the Arsenal players and KSI had to guide Gibbs while I did likewise with Szczęsny, then we switched the blindfolds so that the Playa and KSI were blindfolded. That was just a great night, and it was brilliant when the footballers got what we were doing. Gibbs was more than happy to welcome the hooded wrong 'un that is FIFA Playa into his home.

FIFA Playa even faced off against Spurs and England defender Kyle Walker, who was pretty bewildered to say the least. We played at the *FIFA 14* launch event where Walker and his then teammate Kyle Naughton joined a long list of footballers who had fallen prey to the tantalising skill and confusing charisma of Stevie Scissorhands.

Things got particularly tasty with the aptly named CapgunTom, a YouTube weapons expert, when it was his turn to play the Playa on *Xtreme FIFA*. We had our match in a place the Playa described as a warzone, which was actually a paintball venue (fun fact: this same venue was used again in episode 6 of *The Wembley Cup 2016*), while a paintball gun was being fired at them. When I say 'them', what I really mean is that it was a complete stitch-up. The FIFA Playa must have taken 27 shots to hardly any on CapgunTom. The Playa still managed to win the match and CapgunTom had an apology to deliver, which he did willingly – or at least as willingly as anyone with a paintball gun pointed at them can.

*FIFA* in a paintball warzone was a tough act to follow, but the Playa found himself in far more danger later when *Xtreme FIFA* went to the racetrack – well, the go-karting track, to be precise. In this maximum-velocity game of *FIFA*, Bateson87 and the FIFA Playa would be riding recumbent bicycles (or FIFA Pursuit Vehicles, to give them their technical name) around the circuit, with wireless controllers in their hands, and pursuing a golf buggy (FIFA Utility Kart) with a screen on its back. The driver of the FIFA Utility Kart was none other than superfan, and now sidekick, Thomas Gray.

Keeping up with the buggy was paramount to any kind of success in the game, of course, which presented enough of a physical challenge in itself for those gamers more used to the comfort of the sofa. And to make things more interesting – aside from Thomas Gray's inability to keep his eyes on the road – cardboard-box obstacles were put around the track by the interfering crew. Half-time couldn't come quick enough for the two players.

The second half was a real test of stamina, and when the FIFA Playa sealed a 2–0 victory he celebrated in his own inimitable, cocky style, pedalling around his lap of victory with his hands in the air, giving it large, high-fiving Thomas Gray on the move and daring the crew to throw a cardboard box at him. Which they promptly did.

The box crashed straight into the front of the Playa's kart. He turned into it – a defensive-driving move he might well have learned from thrashing a second-hand Fiat Seicento around in years gone by – and went straight into the front of the golf buggy, which took him clean out, running him over and sending him flying from his bike. He lay battered and broken on the road, while Thomas Gray simply said to the camera, 'Sorry, mate.'

The slow-motion replay confirmed everyone on YouTube's worst fears: it wasn't nearly as bad as it looked. The FIFA Playa was completely fine.

* * *

Wearing a mask was one of the most liberating experiences of my life. It made me fearless. It gave me complete freedom to do what I wanted, to be as ridiculous and embarrassing as possible, but with no comeback because, aside from my friends and family (and, OK, maybe KSI too), no one knew it was me.

Being the FIFA Playa also gave me my first taste of the kind of 'fame' success on YouTube can produce. And it was a really nice kind of fame – the kind with no repercussions in my everyday life.

I remember one amazing moment with it when I went to the EuroGamer exhibition at Earl's Court in London.

I walked through the doors and crossed the floor, saying hello to the odd YouTuber here and there who knew me from behind the scenes on Copa90, but aside from them, no one knew me.

I was there to do a shoot as the FIFA Playa, so I went into the toilets and got changed in the cubicle into the by now all-too-familiar outfit. It was a bit like a comic-book hero getting into costume, and when I walked out of the cubicle I had a real superhero moment. I had all the gear on but my snood was down as I came out, and there was a kid standing at the sink. He stood there looking at me in the mirror, shocked, while the tap was running, and then he turned and fixed his eyes on me. This lad was clearly a fully fledged soldier in the Playa Army. I pulled my mask up, put my finger to my lips and said, 'Shhhh … '

This time when I walked across the floor, hundreds of kids came up to me asking for selfies and autographs. It was just night and day. It was incredible. It wouldn't have happened anywhere other than at a gaming convention, but it still gave me a little taste of what real fame would be like, even if it was also nice to take the mask off at the end of the day and be anonymous once again. I don't think real fame has a similar 'off' switch.

Of course, anonymity came with its own drawbacks. I'd beaten the two-time *FIFA* world champion fair and square during my time as FIFA Playa, but I couldn't shout about it. Did it bother me that my alter ego was getting all the credit?

One thing for sure was that there wasn't much in the way of long-term prospects on YouTube as myself when it was only my secret identity that everyone recognised. If I wanted any kind of future on YouTube without a mask, I'd be starting from scratch all over again.

Working for Copa90 had been amazing – I'd learned so much and been given the opportunity to do things I undoubtedly would have struggled to do solo – and the FIFA Playa remains one of the things I've done that I'm most proud of today. But I still had that itch to make my own content and strike out on my own.

I'd spent the last year building a separate FIFA Playa channel. Copa90 had been good enough to let me use the character on my own channel in a mutually beneficial arrangement: I would get subscribers thanks to the character, and I would push the subscribers towards the main show and give Copa90 a shout-out for anything they were trying to promote.

For that year, I uploaded a video nearly every day. I would finish work, go home, record and then edit the videos of the Playa doing little challenges or playing *FIFA*. I basically had no life outside of that character, but it paid off: I ended up with something like 130,000 subscribers on the channel by the time I quit my full-time role at Copa90.

I think what some people outside of the YouTube community don't always realise is just how much hard work and dedication is involved in building a channel. I'd be up until all hours editing videos and then have to get up for work in the morning. You have to be constantly making and editing content, posting it and engaging with the community. You can't take much of a break from it while you're growing because you'll lose momentum, so you just have to keep going at it. It's relentless, and it's not for everyone. Sure, what ends up on camera often looks more like fun than work, but it still takes a lot out of you.

I can't say I didn't love it, though.

It all came back to the mask. No one knew who I was, so I couldn't really get any other work outside of the FIFA Playa character, which was a problem now that I'd left my normal job behind. I wanted to concentrate on building my own career but FIFA Playa was simultaneously the only success I'd had while being the one thing holding me back. Copa90 had their hands tied in that they couldn't really have me present another show on the channel as it would immediately give away the secret identity of the FIFA Playa. They knew I wanted to do my own thing too, which was becoming more and more clear. The character was theirs – they owned the rights to it as we'd come up with it while working for Copa90 – but surely we could come up with a solution that allowed me to go out alone as Spencer and maintain the integrity of the character – if you can use such a word about the FIFA Playa.

In the end, we decided that removing the FIFA Playa from my channel entirely was the only way to make a clean break. This would then allow me to rebrand my channel as my own. And we did it with a video that took a little inspiration from the Lindsay Lohan film *Parent Trap*, and a touch of *Reservoir Dogs*.

The final FIFA Playa video, and the only one that would remain on my channel in the future, would bring things nicely – and tantalisingly – to a close. FIFA Playa had been kidnapped and tied up by his superfan Thomas Gray, who reveals himself to be less of a superfan than a crazed obsessive determined to find the formula for the perfect *FIFA* YouTuber out of KSI's sweat, Joe Weller's protein shake, NepentheZ's beard, Batson's hair (not from his head) and the final ingredient ... a piece of FIFA Playa's snood.

And who was the guinea pig for this diabolical scheme? Well, that would be me, Spencer. I was zapped into existence, Frankenstein-style, and came face to face with the FIFA Playa for the first and last time. I said, 'This channel isn't big enough for the both of us. I'm taking over.'

And with that, I freed the FIFA Playa and he walked off to disappear into the internet sunset. He'd left something for me to remember him by, however. In a video that only ended up being online for a few days, I had the name for the FIFA Playa's diehard fans, the #PlayaArmy, tattooed to the bottom of my foot as a punishment for losing a FIFA challenge. Not so much a lethal injection, more a permanent inky stain.

And Copa90 have gone from strength to strength since then. No longer making much gaming-related content, they've concentrated on cementing their place within the football community and I must say they've done it tremendously well. It makes me very proud to see how far Copa90 have come since a few of us started working on it in 2012. In my opinion, the football content on Copa90 is now among the finest you can find anywhere today, not just on YouTube

Will the FIFA Playa ever return? When the time comes and he's the hero YouTube needs once more, at least in his own mind, who can say? The FIFA Playa might just rise again ...

As for me, the mask had made me fearless, but I needed the fear once again. It was time to go it alone as Spencer FC.

# 5

# BEING MYSELF: SPENCER FC

So there I was in April 2014, just me, myself and I. Oh, and the 130,000-plus subscribers I'd acquired from having what was originally the FIFA Playa channel.

I'd never monetised the channel previously, but now, as I changed the channel's name to Spencer FC and rebranded it with a new logo, that would all have to change. This would be what I made my living from, and something was very clear to me: if I messed things up as myself and people unsubscribed or lost interest, I would basically be done for. I'd have to go and get another job and be back to square one.

My first task was to hold on to those subscribers. I could have done something similar to what had been on the channel before. I could have done a poor man's FIFA Playa, but I wanted to go in a completely different direction. Just like when I first turned up for the Heybridge Swifts youth team all those years before, I was worried about whether people would like me. But I'd put myself in this position enough times since to know that I had to give it the best go I possibly could; if I smashed it, get in, and if I didn't, well, at least I'd have no regrets.

One of the earliest big decisions I made was to eradicate any trace of foul language from my content. Do I swear in real life? Of course I do sometimes, but it's not a part of me that I wanted to feature in my videos. I wanted to make things more family-friendly and not close any doors on either potential viewers or brands that might take an interest. YouTube is a young person's medium, so why risk losing the younger part of your audience to parental controls? Sometimes it's easy to slip into using swear words for the sake of a cheap gag, but I always felt that if you're relying on using rude language to entertain then you're probably in the wrong game!

While I might have been going in a completely new direction, I wasn't stupid enough to abandon what had been the foundation of the success I'd enjoyed so far on YouTube: the beautiful game of *FIFA*. My online life was completely rooted in this, and it was time to play ball.

One of my first videos as 'Spencer' was part of a *FIFA 14 Road to Glory* series, in which you take a team in Division 10 of Ultimate Team and try to take them up through the divisions to the promised land of Division 1, somewhere only the world's best players get entry to. Lots of other YouTubers did these kind of series, and KSI did some funny ones where he would rap about the players and make it all very comic, but I wanted to apply some geeky football-related rules on mine unique to myself.

The show was called *Forever Blowin'*, after my team West Ham United's club anthem 'I'm Forever Blowing Bubbles'. What made this particular *Road to Glory* different was that I could only do it with players that either currently played for West Ham or had done so in the past.

I brought a few little DIY touches to the show, too, in the form of some props. I took the virtual player cards in *FIFA* and actually printed them off and made real player cards out of them. I would then put them in a pot – called the pot of destiny – and every time I won a game or my opponent 'rage quit' (a pretty self-explanatory method of ending the game) I got to pick a random player to add to my squad out of the pot. If I lost a game, I would lose a player, which would make it even harder to get out of the division.

The pot of destiny was an emptied tube of Slazenger tennis balls. My stagecraft and production values would eventually go up, of course, but like most YouTubers starting out, I was making my videos in my bedroom. In the first *Forever Blowin'* I'm sitting at a desk at the end of my and Alex's bed in a flat we shared with a couple from New Zealand. God knows what they must have thought when they heard me shouting at the top of my voice at random times from my bedroom. To be fair, though, Joe and Lisa were very understanding of my new career path and we couldn't have wished for better flatmates.

It was pretty lo-fi stuff, but I had grander plans – and I did have some skills to back that up. I'd been on internships for television companies like Channel 4, and I'd done plenty of editing and camera work with Copa90 and in my other jobs. I started editing when I was at university, with Windows Movie Maker, which was pretty basic and a great place to start, and then progressed to Sony Vegas. When I started working with production companies I got introduced to Final Cut Pro and then I finally moved over to Adobe Premiere. I had a basic kit, too. I had the Canon 70D, which is the classic YouTube camera with the flip-around screen so you can see yourself while you film and a half-decent microphone.

*Forever Blowin'* offered me a formula that worked well on YouTube. After 25 episodes and falling agonisingly short of my target of winning Division 1 (the West Ham alumni could only take me so far, it turned out), I followed it up with a series called *Once a Lion*, which abided by the same format except that to qualify for the team, a player had to have at least one cap for England.

My team started off being really bad, with some of the worst one-cap wonders to have played for the Three Lions, and I'd gradually build to have a squad with players like Wayne Rooney and Harry Kane up front, as well as legends like Michael Owen. The Slazenger pot of destiny was back, of course.

I even got my parents involved in the channel. My mum played Texan YouTuber Dirty Mike's mum at *FIFA*, though I suspected foul play when Mike's mum scored a wonder goal to win the battle of the mums. I had to give him a whole Team of the Week team for that (they cost a lot of coins, you know, which we'll come to later).

We had a return match, this time the battle of the dads, neither of whom had played *FIFA* before. Perhaps my dad would appreciate just how difficult and worthwhile mastery at *FIFA* was now. My dad got revenge for Mum and beat Dirty Mike's dad on penalties, and he was very pleased indeed – not least because England had actually won a game on penalties for once.

While I might have looked like I was having a ball onscreen, things weren't quite so straightforward behind the scenes. I was working hard on my content pretty much every single day and night. A typical day would see me sitting up editing until 4 or 5am, while poor Alex was trying to sleep in the same room as she had to get up for work in the morning. She had a good job at advertising agency Leo Burnett that she needed to be fresh for every day, and given that I'd been doing pretty much the same thing for a year prior to that with the FIFA Playa, she was incredibly supportive and understanding.

On top of this, Alex and I had a channel we did together, called Spencer & Alex. We'd originally started the channel as a kind of modern-day photo album for ourselves, to document all the great things we'd done together and to look back on when we're old. There were silly little videos on there of things like Alex plucking my nostril hair (seriously, do not try this at home, kids) and some more memorable, travelogue-style stuff like a road-trip around Europe and Alex doing the London triathlon.

Of all the problems to have with the in-laws, however, a joint YouTube channel is certainly a very modern one. Alex's dad is Polish and her mum is a devout Catholic. They're lovely, lovely people, but they're quite traditional and conservative, and I think it's fair to say they weren't massive fans of some of the first videos we put up. They really didn't like one in particular.

We made a video showing Alex's reaction to an infamous video doing the rounds online, which shall remain nameless in the pages of a family-friendly publication such as this. Her parents got the wrong idea and felt I might be exploiting her in some way, making her watch something so upsettingly disgusting, giving little credence to the idea that Alex was perfectly capable of making her own mind up about whether she wanted to watch something like that on our channel.

It wasn't like we were getting the sort of views any kind of exploitation would justify anyway – hardly anyone was watching back then. Looking back at it now, I can understand their concern. They were just looking out for their daughter, who was relatively new to the YouTube world, though my intentions were, of course, honourable.

I would eventually go on to gain their trust and they're fully behind what we do now, but it took time. The only thing I now wonder about is whether they actually watched the infamous video to see how disgusting it was. Now *that* would have made for an interesting reaction video.

We did get some completely unexpected success with one video on our channel, though. We woke up one morning to find a silly video we did called 'How to Annoy Your Boyfriend' had a million views. We couldn't believe it!

I'd had this kind of success with FIFA Playa, but there'd always been a strategy behind those videos, doing collaborations with other YouTubers and maximising our exposure through any means we could. With this, we'd just put it up and thought nothing of it.

It turned out that internet news source *The Daily Dot* had got hold of it and featured it on their website, and to this day we just can't figure out how they found it. We didn't put any clever tags on it or anything – they just randomly came upon it. It didn't turn our channel into an overnight success, but it did give us a decent boost in subscribers and a bit of hope that maybe we could do it again. It reminded me that sometimes good videos just get discovered completely organically – something which seems to happen less and less now as YouTube is unfortunately far from a perfect meritocracy.

Once I was working all the hours I could to make a success of Spencer FC, I needed to sit down with Alex and have what could have been a difficult conversation with her. No, it definitely wasn't the 'It's not you, it's me' conversation, it was more, 'It's not me, it's you.' But I was talking about who was going to edit the Spencer & Alex content, so it wasn't anything *too* dramatic!

I said to her, 'Look, I love doing Spencer & Alex, but I can't edit the videos any more because I'm snowed under with my channel. If you want to continue our stuff, you need to start editing our videos in your own time.'

It was a big ask, as she had her job to go to and she didn't have any experience of editing videos, but I wasn't asking her to do anything I hadn't been prepared to do when I'd had a job. She was up for it. I taught her the basics pretty quickly and I looked over and checked everything she edited, giving her feedback as she went, and she gradually got the hang of it.

As we started to make more and more content and increasingly spent most of our time at home editing, the flat-share was starting to feel too small for our needs, and in the interests of Alex getting a good night's sleep without me sitting on the computer until all hours at night in the room, we made the decision to move out to Hertfordshire where we could afford the non-London rent on a two-bedroom flat (giving us room for a separate office space). Hertfordshire came with the added bonus of being near to where my brother Seb lived, though little did we know then that we'd be so busy during our time living there we'd barely see him.

I was earning just about enough from YouTube to cover my rent and outgoings by then, and Alex was improving as an editor all the time. She'd reached a really good standard by the time we'd been in Hertfordshire for a few months. She hated the commute to London every day, and we talked about her one day quitting her job to come and help me once I was earning enough money to support us.

But how much was enough? If we waited until I was earning the right amount, we might never get there. We realised then that there was something else Alex needed to do that I had been prepared to do before her. We needed to take a gamble: Alex needed to quit her job. Here came the fear again ...

We had enough saved to help us get by for a little while, and that, along with the small amount I was making from my channel, enabled us to come up with a plan: we would smash it for three or four months, working together, and see how we got on. If we couldn't make a go of it, or if we hated working together and being in a relationship at the same time, Alex would go and get another job, but we weren't banking on that. As Hollywood star Will Smith says, 'There's no reason to have a plan B because it distracts from plan A.'

We worked like dogs, every day for a year. We didn't have a single day off, and a day in the life might consist of editing as many as four or five videos in a day, going to meetings, answering loads of emails, filming content or coming up with new ideas.

I was flat out every single day, and Alex was no longer just editing Spencer & Alex content, but stuff for Spencer FC too. We kept that quiet for a long time as we were worried about what people might think about someone who isn't that into football editing football content, but it was *FIFA* content, not pure football, and I was still watching every video and making changes where necessary. Besides, Alex was a really good editor by this stage, and it freed up loads of time for me – time that I could spend pursuing other projects and growing the channel.

When December 2014 rolled around, we embarked on something we would soon come to call Deathcember, and it almost killed us. Not literally, of course, but it took an awful lot out of us.

We did the *Christmas Advent Calendar*, where we uploaded a video every day of me opening a load of Ultimate Team packs, just like the doors of an advent calendar, for the full 25 days of Christmas, plus an extra show for Boxing Day where I played a tournament with the *Advent Calendar* squad I'd created.

Doing this alongside our usual shows meant that for pretty much all of December we were doing two videos a day instead of our usual one, and we barely slept. I must have got about three hours a night for the entire month, and we even had to make a video on Christmas Day. It was great for the channel in terms of views and it was a really fun show, but we kind of hated it at times too, if I'm honest. That might have come across when a very tired version of myself lost two out of three games with the team I'd created, which was sorely lacking in that magic quality of chemistry, and I declared, 'Why would you create a team out of a random group of players that have no association whatsoever?' Bah humbug, indeed.

None of this would stop us doing it all again the following Christmas, of course!

As if the *Advent Calendar* series wasn't enough, I also decided that December would be a good month for me to reinvent the wheel – or at least the TV gameshow *Wheel of Fortune*.

I called my new show *The Wheel of Futune* (with FUT standing for *FIFA* Ultimate Team), and that's pretty much where the similarities with *Wheel of Fortune* ended – though, in the spirit of producing physical props, which had been a feature of my shows so far, we did have a homemade wheel. Alex put a lot of tender loving care into crafting and painting that bad boy, and it's still going strong after three seasons!

The production values were going up. I dressed up in my best showbiz-presenter/circus-performer garb to present the first episode. OK, we weren't able to match the levels of a real-life TV gameshow – 'We didn't have the budget for that,' I pointed out in the first episode – but I felt we could become a nice middle ground between a typical YouTube video and a well-produced entertainment series on TV.

The premise of the show was that I would spin the wheel before every match, and wherever it landed I would have to obey the command for my next *FIFA* match. So, some parts of the wheel offered me the opportunity to open player packs, which might include some good players to add to my squad and would obviously help me in the game, and some allowed me to buy players. But other parts of the wheel meant I had to do a challenge or I would be made bankrupt. The only players I could use throughout the series were those the wheel gave me.

These restrictions made my target to win Division 1 harder, not least because the players I would be up against were playing the game with nothing inhibiting them. Now, I'm a decent *FIFA* player – I'm not world-class by any means, but I'm not bad – which allowed me to achieve some epic victories against good players who had their best team and no restrictions on them. It might have taken 48 episodes, over 250 players and nearly 150 spins of the wheel, but in my first series I achieved my target of winning Division 1.

Some of the challenges the wheel might make me do included playing with a team that had zero chemistry (meaning the players had no links to each other, which inhibited their on-pitch performance) or with everyone out of position (so that I would have a goalkeeper up front and a striker in goal), and every now and then I'd sneak a 1–0 victory against a decent team. I loved it when that happened!

And my loving it was, I felt, where the real heart of the show lay. By the time I was doing *The Wheel of Futune* I was getting decent subscriber numbers. In fact, I was picking them up quicker than before. Any worries I'd had about replacing FIFA Playa with the more family-friendly version of myself were long gone.

I wasn't achieving this through chasing viewers and working out tactics to bump up subscriber numbers. I was making series that I genuinely enjoyed because I knew my passion would come through in the content. Unfortunately, there's a lot of fake stuff on YouTube – fake reactions, fake enthusiasm, fake people – but I can hold my hand on my heart and say that I've never faked a single thing. Every ounce of excitement and enthusiasm you see in my content is 100 per cent real. When you see me celebrate a goal or 'packing' a great player, that's genuine.

As I've said before, I'm not one for faking enthusiasm, and the fact that I'm still making *The Wheel of Futune* videos today should tell you a little something about just how much I enjoy it. Regardless of view counts or comments, if I ever stop enjoying something I stop doing it. I've proven this with the jobs I left earlier in my career and it's part of my personality that I don't see changing.

If I could pinpoint any single factor in the success of Spencer FC, it would be that year that Alex and I spent putting in such a shift. But that really isn't unique on YouTube. If you look at anyone with any degree of success on the platform, the one thing the majority have in common is that they work hard. Even if you don't like their content, most creators will still have had to work hard to get to where they are. It isn't always easy to appreciate that, but most YouTubers are all too familiar with some very late nights to keep putting out the content that we do.

What was pretty unique about the work Alex and I were putting in was that we were doing it together while being in a relationship. Now, guys, I can tell you right now that it could have gone very wrong. Very wrong indeed. Working every day without a break with your partner isn't exactly the best foundation for a relationship, as every stress and every strain from both the work and the relationship filter over and affect both sides of it. For the wrong couple, even with a solid-as-a-rock relationship, it could have been horrible. If you asked my mum and dad if they could manage working full-time together, you'd get a very strong 'NO WAY' in response!

Thankfully, we managed it pretty well. I'm not going to say there weren't fraught moments, but during that year we learned that we could work together and live together and keep our relationship strong. We had no choice but to commit to it all, and thankfully it started paying off. Within six months we were making more than enough to pay our rent, and within a year we would move to a bigger place. But, most importantly, securing our finances and making a success of the channel meant I was able to make the content I wanted with the production values I'd envisaged at the start.

I can never give Alex enough credit for how much she helped me and allowed me to chase my dreams. Who knows what would have happened if she'd said 'no thanks' when I asked her to start editing Spencer & Alex videos back in the day? The fact is she jumped on board and her commitment, enthusiasm and tireless work ethic are some of the main reasons I'm here writing this book. She is a gamechanger.

• • •

One route I could have pursued to make life easier and to get the money coming in quicker would have been to have a *FIFA* coin sponsor on my channel, but I made the decision very early on to turn my back on this form of income.

In *FIFA* Ultimate Team, you can use in-game coins to buy better players. You can earn these coins gradually through playing the game, or you can speed up the process by paying real money – dipping into your own pocket – to buy *FIFA* points from the makers of the game, EA Sports.

Now, the points are expensive to buy, especially if you've already shelled out the not-insignificant sum for the game itself, so naturally, as is always the way in any economy, especially on the internet, some enterprising people found a way to hack the system and sell the coins themselves – at a heavily discounted rate.

This practice was illegal as it was effectively undercutting the people who owned the rights to the currency (EA Sports), but the appeal was simple: cheaper in-game coins. To think of it in old money, imagine a Panini football sticker book filled with fake stickers bought from a guy on the street rather than the official manufacturers.

These enterprising people took a similarly novel approach to their marketing strategy: they paid to have links to their websites advertised on the channels of prominent *FIFA* YouTubers. And they paid a lot of money to do it with YouTubers who had millions of subscribers – all potential customers.

For a couple of years, some YouTubers got incredibly rich from doing this. We're talking tens of thousands of pounds a month. I could have been earning this kind of money, and lots of YouTubers I know were, and fair play to them, it's not my place to judge. You might think me mad not to, given the struggle Alex and I went through to make a success of the channel, but I made the decision when *FIFA 15* came out that I wouldn't be accepting a coin sponsor, and I did it for a couple of reasons.

Firstly, EA were starting to crack down on it and punish people who bought the black-market coins. I didn't feel comfortable advertising something that could get one of my viewers into trouble. 'Spencer told me to do it,' they'd say, and who could blame them? I didn't think it would be a responsible thing for me in the long term to put my viewers in that position.

Secondly, EA were beginning to punish the people advertising coin sellers too. So, yes, in the interests of self-preservation, I didn't want my account getting shut down or to be forced to stop one of my *Road to Glory* series short. These series were my lifeblood at the time and part of the story I was telling on YouTube.

The third reason was one that I wasn't entirely confident of at the time but I was growing to understand. I felt there was a chance that being associated with this murky illegitimate industry may have an adverse effect on me later down the line. This wasn't a career path in which I wanted to just dip my feet in, get rich quick and then move on to something else. This was something I wanted to do for the rest of my life, and I didn't think the potential risks outweighed the obvious benefits.

And above all else, quite simply, I didn't need a coin sponsor. I was able to make content I was really happy with that got a good amount of views without one, and I would eventually be able to make a reasonable income on my own terms. Sure, I wouldn't be buying a flash sports car or a penthouse apartment any time soon, but that was never why I did this. I wanted to be able to make ends meet, that was all, and by the time *FIFA 15* came around I could.

My stand on the issue paid off in the long run. I was one of the first YouTubers to work with EA, and that partly came about because they hadn't blacklisted me for having a coin sponsor (although I hope it mainly came about because they thought I was pretty good!).

Because of that decision, I've got to do some pretty amazing things with the company. I was the first person from the YouTube community to go into the actual game when I became the voice of the *FIFA 16* tutorials. I have gone to Real Madrid and played the players at *FIFA*, same with Chelsea, and I was part of the presenting team that hosted both the *FIFA 16* and the *FIFA 17* launch events, which, for the kid who used to slide the mouse off the table while he lost to his older brother at the game time and time again, were amazing moments.

I didn't know my choice would lead to all these things, though, as it was a fair while after I'd done it that EA approached me. That didn't stop some people giving me stick for it. Because of the negative opinion some people in the community held of EA Sports due to their very expensive in-game currency and various technical issues still prevalent in the game, I was labelled a 'sell-out' by some ill-informed *FIFA* fans despite the fact that I did things the hard way by not taking the coin-sponsor money and instead scraping and saving to make my way at the beginning.

The irony was that I'd never received a penny from EA at this point either! It wasn't until years later, in 2017, when I was honoured to be made part of the *FIFA* Ultimate Team eSports presenting team; that I actually did my first paid job for the company.

My feelings about the price of *FIFA* points themselves weren't complicated. Yes, they were expensive, and I could understand people feeling frustrated with that. I was using *FIFA* on my channel so I could justify the expenditure on them, but if I was playing just as a punter, as I had for so many years before, would I have felt comfortable shelling out for them?

I probably wouldn't. So there's the answer as I see it: if you think they're too expensive, stop buying them. If everyone made a real protest and stopped buying them, then the price would have to fall – it's just simple economics. It's the same thing I think every time Arsenal fans complain about the cost of their tickets. If they're too expensive, stop buying them. As long as people are willing to continue paying more for them, the price is always going to go up. It's business – and unfortunately that's what football at the top level is now. The only thing that will prompt clubs to take action is an empty stadium, because no business wants to lose money.

● ● ●

*FIFA* content was serving me well and was the backbone of the channel, but with Alex aboard I was more able to spread out into the area I really wanted to when I first conceived of the channel. I had always planned to make football content, not just *FIFA*, when I called it Spencer FC. I could have just called it Spencer Gaming HD if that had been the limit of my plans. I no longer worried about what anyone might think about the kid who got into football late voicing his opinions.

I started putting some football opinion pieces in among the *FIFA* content, and some silly sketch videos about transfer deadline day. I started a series called *IMO* (*In My Opinion*), which consisted purely of me sharing my opinion on various controversial football stories. I created my own YouTube

Football panel show called *Bench Warmers*. I even started a football podcast.

Alex and I were still working all the hours and more that we could in our pressure cooker of a Hertfordshire flat, but we'd settled into a good groove by this point and I was even finding some release by playing Sunday league football every week.

While I'd been living in London I'd played a lot of five- and seven-a-side football, but playing Sunday league had fallen away a little bit as I didn't really have a team in the capital. Moving back to Hertfordshire meant I could more easily hook up with my old uni mate Rich Beck, whose dad ran the team Taplow Swans near Maidenhead in Buckinghamshire. I'd played for Taplow for three seasons at university and I was able to slip back into the team now, four years later. Playing for them was a highlight of the week for me, though it wasn't without its pitfalls.

During one match for them, I decided to try to tackle someone with my face. Not my brightest idea. As I was making videos every day for Spencer FC, I had a black eye for about three-and-a-half weeks' worth of content. When I played MiniMinter – a member of one of the UK's biggest YouTube groups, the Sidemen – for my series *Football vs FIFA*, my shiner was there in all its glory for every one of the 3.5 million viewers to see (what did I tell you about collaborations?).

I was starting to play a bit of football on Spencer FC, too. I didn't just play Simon (MiniMinter's real name) at *FIFA*. One part of the *Football vs FIFA* series consisted of a real-life best-of-six football challenge, in which we would compete in a penalty shootout, a free-kick challenge, hitting the crossbar from outside the box, scoring direct from a corner kick, kick-ups and lobbing the goalkeeper. The goalkeeper would be my brother Seb.

Any thoughts that I might enjoy a bit of fraternal help soon went out the window when Seb managed to make his first save of the penalty shootout against one of mine! And when Seb allowed Simon to do a cheeky chip on him in the free-kick challenge, all I could say was, 'Sebby, what are you doing to me?'

Simon beat me 4–2 on the football challenges, which meant he got a four-star team and I would play with a two-star team at *FIFA*. Simon rubbed salt in my wounds by going with my beloved West Ham, while I chose Bradford City, rivals of the team he supports, Leeds United. Defeat would hurt that little bit more for the loser.

I somehow managed to draw the match 2–2, thanks to a calamitous own goal from Simon – the only time I'm likely to ever celebrate such a mix-up at the back for West Ham – and I had my revenge for the real-life penalties earlier when I beat Simon in the penalty shootout afterwards. The black eye wasn't smarting quite so much by then.

Following this, *Football vs FIFA* would see me go up against many other worthy opponents such as my brother Seb in the next episode. At least that meant I wouldn't have to put up with his dodgy keeper skills. It didn't make much difference, though, as Seb beat me by the same score in the football challenge that Simon had. We had a wrong-footed penalty shootout, and I thought all my years being right-footed but playing at left-back would come in handy, but I lost that challenge too!

Once again, though, the *FIFA* section gave me a chance for redemption and the results probably weren't too unexpected: while the student was definitely now the master at the video game, Seb's real football skills were a different matter entirely. Maybe I should have got a headers challenge in there, too.

I kept the *FIFA* series coming, with things like *The Zarate Kid*, in which I attempted a kind of anti-*Road to Glory* challenge, where I would actually start in Division 1, where all the best players and teams were, and attempt to win it, but I had such a weak team that it would be more like a relegation battle than a triumphant title cakewalk.

The twist in this show was that the one permanent fixture in my team had to be maverick West Ham striker Mauro Zárate, and my bonuses involved Zárate scoring goals, getting assists or winning man of the match. Understandably, my number-one attacking tactic was simply to get the ball to Zárate.

In the spirit of the *Karate Kid* pun in the title of the show, I wore a karate outfit throughout the series and made plenty of dubious kung-fu sound effects. Game on!

This kind of flippant *FIFA* fun was in marked contrast to an assignment I took on from my friends at Copa90 to make the kind of content that could never be described as just some young YouTuber hiding out in their bedroom making videos.

The Copa90 guys sent me and one of their presenters, a good friend of mine called Eli Mengem, out to Bosnia and Herzegovina to report on the biggest derby in their league between two teams from the capital city, FK Sarajevo and FK Željezničar. Eli had been to the game before, and he had no hesitation in spelling out just what a crazy fixture it was.

Everything around the game certainly backed that up, as firstly we enjoyed a ride from the airport with a taxi driver who was a bit of a nutcase, and then we went to check out FK Sarajevo's stadium the day before the match. There, we witnessed a supporter of one Sarajevo team propose to his girlfriend, who supported the opposing derby team, in the empty stadium. It was pretty *Romeo and Juliet*, with two competing families/ football teams coming together through the power of love. Though I thought the whole point of proposing in a sports arena was to do it in front of a huge crowd!

Still, he lit a flare, which I would soon learn was very much the thing to do in this stadium, got down on one knee and she said yes. That was worthy of a cheer from Eli and me.

Evidence of the troubles this city had endured in its turbulent past were apparent all over the place in the form of bullet holes. And on match day, as the ultras gathered, lit their flares and marched the streets, there was a whiff of conflict in the air once again when the police lined up against them.

This was no ordinary derby. The two teams were fighting for the title. The stadium had nets up to stop people in the crowd throwing stuff, and once the match got started it became clear how pointless a gesture this was. Eli and I stood filming on the running track, pitch-side, when people in the crowd started throwing flares towards us. Smoke quickly covered the pitch and the match had to be paused, but that was only part of the madness.

Željezničar were nicknamed the Smurfs, and some FK Sarajevo fans were burning and biting the heads off stuffed-toy Smurfs. Some people were climbing the poles that held up the crowd nets. Flares were landing by our feet. It was madness – this was football reporting from the front line. This was *Ross Kemp on Gangs* stuff.

But would I do it again? You bet I would. It was great to work with the Copa90 guys again, and the atmosphere, while intimidating, was just sensational. My YouTube channel was opening doors I'd never thought possible before, and I was desperate to take advantage of them all.

I was already enjoying a taste of club ownership after buying shares in Spanish club Real Oviedo a couple of years previously, when they had fallen on hard times and been relegated to the third tier of the Spanish league system. When they made an appeal to the football community, people responded from across the world, and it brought genuine football fans together in an amazing effort to save this unique football club, raising millions of pounds in the process.

This time, in 2015, they were launching another appeal for funds. Unlike other clubs that might sell their shares expensively, the shares in Real Oviedo were going for the very reasonable price of €11.50 each, so I thought it was a great idea to share the opportunity with my viewers. Crowdsourcing can be a wonderful thing when it brings the fans together and helps a club that once had players like Juan Mata, Santi Cazorla and Michu in their ranks and wants genuine football lovers involved. It meant I would be co-owner of a club along with my viewers, and we would all have a genuine second team to support together.

Going out to Oviedo for some of their big promotion-push games remains a highlight for me. The atmosphere was always electric and the fans were incredibly welcoming.

Seeing Real Oviedo win promotion back to the second tier of Spanish football was not only one of my favourite moments in my career, but also as a football fan in general. I've been lucky enough to meet the squad, the staff and even collaborate with the team for my very own Real Oviedo Career Mode on *FIFA 16*, which featured the actual players popping up in my content from time to time.

During all of this, my channel hit a real milestone: half-a-million subscribers. It was an incredible moment not just for me, but for Alex too, as I simply couldn't have done it without her help and support. From where we'd started out, inheriting 130,000 subscribers from the FIFA Playa and not only holding on to those viewers, but almost quadrupling them in less than a year was an achievement I was just so proud of.

Sure, half-a-million subscribers was small change for some of the biggest YouTubers whose subscribers number in the millions, but from where I'd come from, to have worked as hard as we had and to have done it all on my own terms was so, so special, and I was incredibly grateful to everyone who had tuned in, commented and enjoyed my content – and I hope plenty of you guys are reading this now. It's a team effort and I genuinely treasure every one of my subscribers.

I created a Draw My Life video to celebrate the achievement, a kind of truncated video version of this book so far, if you like (but don't put this down and watch that instead just yet – there's plenty more to come in this book!). And, given the reflective nature of a Draw My Life video, it felt like a pretty good time for me to take stock of how I'd got here.

I knew my passion had played a major role, and I'd always believed that if I did something I loved on YouTube, it would come across and people would want to watch.

Hard work had played its part too. But, as I'd found when I was made captain temporarily for Heybridge Swifts' youth team years before, the right attitude will only take you so far. Sure, I'd worked hard, but so had everyone else who had enjoyed some consistent success on YouTube.

The thing I kept coming back to was the fact that, at the ripe old age of 26, I was actually pretty old for a YouTuber, certainly compared to the 16- and 17-year-olds putting out videos. That meant I had a whole host of references and influences to be inspired by that wouldn't necessarily be available to these other guys.

I'd come of age at a period in time when the internet was only just coming of age, which meant I'd grown up watching programmes like *Blue Peter* and *Art Attack* on an actual television set (remember that old metal box that your furniture used to point at?). My real inspiration didn't come from other YouTubers, because YouTube was never around for me to be inspired by. It came from television and movies and music and books, which inspired ideas for things like *The Wheel of Futune* and *The Zarate Kid*. It's not that I was coming up with anything staggeringly original every time, more that I was able to provide a fresh twist on *FIFA* series using the influences that mattered to me.

And being a few years older than many of the other YouTubers also meant that I was a few years into my career. I had learned production values from television jobs, and stagecraft from presenting and stand-up comedy gigs. I was committed to YouTube long before it was ever a career option for me, and I think achieving this level of success relatively late meant that I was better able to handle it.

It must be really tempting and all too easy for a teenage YouTuber who achieves success quickly to think, *Well, that was easy: I've smashed life, got a load of money in the bank – now what?*

It's why I really admire the young guys who keep going, who keep working at it, because I can't say with absolute certainty whether that would have been me. I think for some people, success can come a bit too soon. You only have to look at some of the forgotten teenage superstars in professional football to see that happen all too frequently.

I certainly wasn't satisfied with resting on my laurels. Having busted a gut to get to this point, I was already thinking about the next half-million subscribers. And I had a plan so secret, so cunning and so unbelievably exciting that I just couldn't wait to share it with my viewers.

I visited the West Ham United office in Westfield, Stratford, at the start of summer 2015 to choose my season-ticket seats for the 2016–17 season, the first that West Ham would play in their incredible new home, the Olympic Stadium in East London.

But the Olympic Stadium was nothing compared to what I had planned next.

# 6

# THE ROAD TO WEMBLEY

Back in 2013, when the identity of a certain FIFA Playa was still a hot topic on YouTube, Copa90 put on a football tournament featuring the cream of YouTube talent – and FIFA Playa. In the final of the Copa90 Cup, a team of YouTube Allstars took on the Copa90 team, with people like KSI, Poet and MiniMinter on the pitch. Unbelievably, Copa90 turned their noses up at the opportunity to have Stevie Two Shoes on their team, and he turned out for the Allstars instead.

The match was played in quite low-key surroundings and was settled on penalties, with the Allstars taking the glory. But the result wasn't what was important – or at least it wasn't once FIFA Playa stopped gloating about it. What was important was that it whetted the appetite for a proper YouTube football match.

At the 2014 Gamescom, a huge video-game trade fair in Cologne, Germany, I hung out with a lot of these guys and we got chatting about how cool it would be to play football together. With the packed schedules we all had and the absolute nightmare it would be to synchronise a good period of time for us to play together, that's all it really felt like to most of the guys, just idle chat and pipe dreams.

Except it wasn't for me.

I said to the boys, 'Look, I am going to try to make this happen. If I get it organised, will you be up for it?'

They said, 'Yeah – if you can sort it, we'll be there.'

I left Gamescom that year feeling really motivated that I could put something together, though little did I realise then that it would be the best part of a year and an unbelievable amount of hard work before my idea came to fruition.

Playing football is the ultimate for me. I love making content about football, love watching football and playing football computer games, but playing the game is still the most enjoyable thing I can do. You tell me where there's a game on and I'm there. And the possibility of combining playing the game with the content I was already making just seemed too good an opportunity to pass up. In September 2014, I started pitching a YouTuber football match.

I had some good contacts at YouTube, not only from my old job at Copa90 but from the content I was making for my own channel, which I'd only been doing for a few months by this stage. I'd worked with brands before, so I knew what they'd want, and I also had the YouTuber mindset: I understood what the other guys would want to get out of something like this.

Traditionally, a brand will approach a YouTuber and offer to pay them to promote their campaign, but what I was doing was approaching a brand with an idea I wanted to do that would require their investment – and no little amount of trust, too.

YouTube loved the idea, and we took it to various digital agencies to try to get them onboard. The idea that we originally pitched was very different from the event we would end up creating. We wanted to create a full, 11-a-side football team with YouTubers, in which we would fly out to a tournament somewhere glamorous like Las Vegas and make a bit of a reality TV show out of it, filming us playing football and having plenty of fun off the pitch too.

An agency called Poke really liked the basis of the idea, but they proposed a different way of doing things. There was one particular brand that they worked with whom they felt would be the perfect catalyst for this project. Mobile phone and broadband provider EE might not have got on board with a lads' jolly to Las Vegas, but they had something else at their disposal, something even better than an all-expenses-paid trip to the party capital of the world. They had Wembley Stadium.

With Poke and EE, official sponsors of Wembley Stadium, onboard, it was up to me to go away and create an idea and develop a series around a match at Wembley Stadium, the home of football. I could hardly believe my luck.

The idea I came up with was that I would create a team, called Spencer FC after my channel, that would take on a Sidemen team. The Sidemen are the conglomerate of huge UK YouTubers headed up by KSI, and their team would be called Sidemen United. The prize at stake for both teams? The inaugural Wembley Cup.

The show was almost a year in the making. I put a load of work into planning, producing and coming up with the ideas for the series, alongside some of Poke's very talented creatives. This is where I really enjoyed the benefits of Alex being at home editing the content I'd filmed the night before and uploading it to YouTube for my channel. It allowed me to be able to attend so many meetings and work all-out on the Wembley Cup. Alex was absolutely integral to this, and her role cannot be understated.

One early stumbling block came in the form of the involvement of YouTube's biggest star. EE were concerned about the nature of KSI's content at the time, specifically the fact that it wasn't the kind of stuff every parent was likely to want to let their young, impressionable children watch. It was looking like KSI might not be allowed to play.

Now, JJ (KSI) won't mind me saying this (or at least I hope he won't), but some of the content he has made isn't the kind of stuff I'd put on my channel. On Spencer FC I don't swear and I try to make it as family-friendly as possible, so everyone can watch and parents can relax about it. I do things in a way I believe to be the right one for me, but who's to say whose approach is right? KSI can just as easily point to his 16 million subscribers and the massive success he's enjoyed to claim the high ground!

There were a couple of reasons that I really wanted JJ to play. Firstly because he's a good mate who has not only been very generous to me over the years, but also paved the way for all of us to do what we do. Make no mistake, without KSI being one of the first people to prove there was both demand and a way of making a living from *FIFA* content, there would be no Spencer FC, at least not in the sense that it exists now.

Secondly, and perhaps obviously, I really wanted JJ to play because of the huge appeal he and his audience would bring to the show. He was part of the motivation for wanting to do the series in the first place, and the idea of doing it without him didn't feel right. I felt so strongly, in fact, that at one point I said I might walk away from the show if he couldn't play.

We reached a bit of an impasse, but in the end, KSI being KSI and all the commitments on his time that entailed, he couldn't do the dates anyway because he was going out to LA to shoot a movie. Typical! We dodged a bullet on that one. To this day I'm not entirely sure what would have happened if JJ hadn't had his movie shoot at the same time. Maybe there would have never been a Wembley Cup!

So with him making his peace with not being involved and me doing likewise, we got the rest of the Sidemen on board as well as some other huge YouTubers, including the F2 Freestylers, ChrisMD and Joe Weller, and the show went on.

Of course, getting the cream of YouTube footballers to give up their time not just for a match at Wembley, but for an entire series based around that match, was never going to come cheap, and I certainly didn't have the kind of funds necessary, so EE had to pay everyone involved. That's only right: once a brand is involved, you shouldn't be expected to do something for free.

Putting together something of this magnitude for my channel was a real learning curve not only for me, but for everyone involved in the project. When one of the YouTubers was playing hardball over his fee – which he had every right to do, of course – one of the senior executives involved said something that frustrated me a little. He said, 'I don't get it, if someone had offered me the chance to play at Wembley when I was eighteen, I would have loved it.'

Now, don't get me wrong, of course the prospect of playing at Wembley is every football fan's dream, but it's impossible to compare a normal young adult with the guys we had involved in this project. The only way that was even remotely a valid comparison was if this person had a million fans and all the trappings of self-made success when he was 18, which he clearly hadn't. If it had just been a match at Wembley, I'm sure loads of them would have played for free, but there were multiple shoots as well as brand endorsement to commit to as well.

The brand were paying for the kind of reach these guys had for the good of their company. This was an emerging generation of a new type of celebrity, and expecting them to take time out of their diary to commit to a brand for free was just never going to happen. They wouldn't have expected any other kind of 'mainstream celebrity' to do that. Saying what he did was a bit like saying I could have been great at snooker instead of *FIFA*: it was that generational divide once again.

To give them their due, everyone at EE learned from the experience and they were fantastic – really brilliant to work with. And I had plenty of learning to do too on the series. Meetings, mapping out the episodes and the diary management of a group of highly successful workaholic young men on a series with production values far beyond the scope of anything I'd attempted on my channel so far all ensured that I was kept on my toes throughout.

I loved every minute of it. Thanks to the kind of funds that EE invested, we were able to make a production unlike anything that had been seen on YouTube before, at least not in our genre. Even on the episodes leading up to the match itself, we had 20-man crews and TV-worthy production values. A brand like EE aren't going to spend that amount of money on something that looks naff, and the whole series was up there in their production budget alongside their TV adverts.

The first episode, however, started off on pretty familiar turf. MiniMinter and I had an Ultimate Rematch on *FIFA* after our *Football vs FIFA* head-to-head previously on my channel. I'd just beaten him that time, but this particular member of the Sidemen was out for revenge. In a match-up of teams that had brought tears to my eyes all the way back in 1998 when they played for real, it was time for my England team to play his Argentina.

It was no contest, really. He thrashed me 3–0 as I not only let myself down, but I let my country down too. There were no tears this time, though, as I turned to him and said, 'Enough of this nonsense. Let's settle this properly. Proper football, me versus you. I'll make a team of YouTubers, you make a team of YouTubers. We'll settle it on the pitch, son.'

'Alright,' MiniMinter said. 'Let's do it.'

It was game on for Spencer FC vs Sidemen United.

The next episode saw me recruit my vice-captain, Joe Weller, who is a good pal and a very successful YouTuber. We had a bit of a bonding session and wrestled with some of the big decisions we'd need to make for the team, like the kit design. We settled on something that was, in his words, 'very, very sexy' and a bit 'tropical'. We even found time to channel our inner Ryan Giggs and get a cheeky yoga session in.

Joe was the second name on the team sheet, after me, of course. I'd put myself down for a central-midfield role and Joe was ready to lead the line up top. My team was starting to come together.

Next up, I had to find a midfielder for the team to complement my more defensive approach to the game. Wembley's a big pitch, and I needed someone who could spray the passes accurately around it. I was all too aware that I was not that player.

The best and most entertaining way that I could see to find such a player was to have a FootGolf competition – playing 'golf' with a football, you will be unsurprised to learn. It was a bit of a new sport that people were talking about, so it seemed like a good idea for a video. I lined up some top YouTubers to compete for the position: Hurder Of Buffalo aka George Benson, ChrisMD and Manny.

George started very strongly indeed, making a very decent case for a starting place at Wembley. I made a pretty strong case myself as I managed a hole in one! This wasn't about me, though. It was about finding another player for the team. But I still think it's worth mentioning here, in print, just to be clear: *I got a hole in one.*

ChrisMD came out on top and secured his place as playmaker in the middle of the park, but just as we were congratulating him, I received a video message from my rival captain, MiniMinter.

But it wasn't Simon who was doing the talking on the video – it was none other than former professional footballer and manager Ray Wilkins. He was in the process of signing a contract to manage the Sidemen team, and he had something to say.

'You'll need a bit more than FootGolf to beat our lads,' he said. 'I'm sure we're going to turn you over because we're in it to win it.'

Strong words indeed that perhaps underestimated the range of skills and football brain required to excel at a fast-growing sport like FootGolf. Would he have said something like that if he'd seen my hole in one? Whatever. The Sidemen were coming for us, and it was time to up the stakes.

We needed a big man at the back to be the heart of the defence, commanding things. So we built a pretty epic assault course to put NepentheZ, Poet, AnEsonGib and Vujanic through their paces and find our starting centre-back for Wembley.

First up was the water jump, where Vujanic did his chances no favours at all by chickening out of it – because he didn't want to get wet! What would a hardened central defender like Bobby Moore or Vincent Kompany do in the same position?

They then clambered through a truck, turned over tractor tyres in a test of strength and climbed over several obstacles. They were a long way from home right now, and some of the guys were struggling without a controller in their hands or a comfortable chair to sit in. Nobody ever said the road to Wembley would be easy.

The course had certainly taken its toll by the end. 'I'm actually dead, mate,' said NepentheZ, while Vujanic, who had carried a twig around pretending it was a gun in just one of a string of eccentric incidents on the day, proudly declared, 'I didn't get wet.'

Poet was the victor on the day, and he celebrated with a rap. All of which meant we not only had a tall, composed defender, but we had one who could talk a good game too.

When it was time to find a striker to partner Joe Weller up front, we were getting ever closer to Wembley. Literally, as it turned out: we did our centre-forward trials on a pitch overlooking the hallowed turf of our national stadium. If that didn't inspire our wannabe goal poachers, I didn't know what would.

Fighting it out for the centre-forward berth were the F2 Freestylers (Billy Wingrove and Jeremy Lynch), Burnt Chip and RossiHD. With all due respect to Chip and Rossi, I didn't envy them taking on the F2 boys. They have some serious skills and, while being a great freestyler doesn't always translate into being a brilliant player, these guys could do the lot.

As we were aiming to take the Sidemen down, we set up a target practice in which our contestants would be aiming at targets made out of the Sidemen's faces, with MiniMinter's lovely mug presenting the real jackpot, at the back in the goal. To give the guys some expert advice, we had none other than the Southampton and England legend that is Matt Le Tissier. He preached the values of being cool under pressure and visualising where you wanted the ball to go.

RossiHD got a solid start, knocking the block off a couple of close-range Sidemen, but Billy really upped the stakes with a perfect bull's-eye on MiniMinter's face. What a shot!

'Sorry, Simon,' Billy said with the decapitated cardboard head of MiniMinter under his arm. 'When you're worth a hundred points, you're going down, mate.'

The Burnt Chip and even fellow F2 boy Jeremy couldn't match Billy's score, so we had our striker. I just hoped that Billy and Joe could form a solid partnership up top.

Having not fancied swapping places with the boys taking on the F2 Freestylers, I then put myself in an even more unenviable position by taking on Matt Le Tissier himself. Now, if you're too young to remember Matt playing, go check out some of the goals he scored on YouTube. The man could seriously strike a ball from some outrageous positions, and I was about to find out that you never really lose it.

'It's been thirteen years since I retired,' he said, 'so you must be in with a chance.'

Ha!

His first couple of strikes were just range-finders, shaking off the dust of those 13 years in retirement, before he curled the kind of absolute beauty he was worshipped for at Southampton straight into MiniMinter's face. Jackpot time! His score was better even than Billy's.

I just couldn't live with skills that decent, and I was more than happy to admit defeat to the man who very much still had it. Even now, after having done football-related videos with many current and ex-footballers, I have to say that Matt impressed me massively on the day.

Class is permanent.

To choose another central defender, the guys got to actually play at Wembley. Play *FIFA*, that is. We had a major international *FIFA* tournament among six of our brightest YouTube stars in a box at the stadium, and AnEsonGib, who had been denied in the assault-course episode, came good in a penalty shootout against NepentheZ.

His prize wasn't just a starting place at Wembley, however. He also got to play a game of *FIFA* against someone who was no stranger to the real Wembley turf: Spurs and England winger Andros Townsend. AnEsonGib, controlling Argentina, might have had the *FIFA* skills, but Andros (who now plays for Crystal Palace), unsurprisingly controlling England, had the big-match experience and he was unlikely to be fazed by the occasion at Wembley. Unbelievably, Andros, who was a great sport on the day, came out on top after penalties. England winning a penalty shootout? Only on *FIFA*!

Now, no team is complete without a couple of first-class wide men, and we'd need some cheeky wingcraft to serve our forwards Joe Weller and Billy Wingrove. You could say we'd need good wide men to beat the Sidemen ... I'll get my coat.

We headed to St George's Park, Burton, home to the England national teams, to find our pacy wingers. We took a load of top YouTube talent to the gym to warm up, then we headed to one of the training pitches where Melissa Lawley, an England women's team striker, and Mike Thorpe, an FA coach, would put them through their paces.

First up was a dribbling challenge where we'd all have to try and take a ball through a variety of obstacles, using close control against the clock. Unsurprisingly, F2 Freestyler Jeremy Lynch demonstrated the skills that pay his bills with a seriously fast time, while Manny's crowd-pleasing flair certainly caught the eye – and earned a deserved round of applause from the lads. Twinkle-toes Jeremy and trickster Manny had done enough to be my wide men for the final.

With just the goalkeeper and the two full-back positions vacant for the final, our squad played our first ever match together to see how the team gelled. Our opponents were Dodgy Barnet United, a team made up of employees from Poke and EE, and they clearly had a bit more of that much-needed quality chemistry, at least to start with, as they raced into a 2–0 lead. But that twinkle-toed man Jeremy nicked us a goal before half-time, which is always a great time to get back into a game ...

Especially given that we had Arsenal legend Martin Keown in our dugout. Having seen the Sidemen recruit Ray Wilkins, I knew we needed someone of equal stature to manage our side, and who better than one of the Invincibles himself? Martin's half-time team talk helped us go out in the second half and fight back to win the game 5–3. And now it was time to pick the last three positions.

They say you have to be a bit mad to be a goalkeeper, and Vujanic certainly fitted that description. His safe hands ensured he would be wearing the gloves. Our left-back would be George Benson, while shoring up the right side of defence would be the less-experienced but super-keen Oakelfish. We had our team.

What we didn't yet have, of course, was our team song. No trip to Wembley would be complete without a suitable cup-final single, so Poet, Joe Weller, Vujanic and I headed to the studio along with super-producer Brett Domino to lay down the Spencer FC anthem.

It was very much a Live Aid atmosphere down in the studio, and I think it's fair to say that not since Spurs legends Glenn Hoddle and Chris Waddle graced the charts with their legendary version of 'Diamond Lights' (look it up on YouTube) had there ever been such a perfect marriage between beautiful game and popular song.

Unfortunately, when I did a quick search for the lyrics of our song online, I couldn't find them on any of the usual internet song-lyric providers, which is a disgrace if you ask me. Don't worry, though. I remember them. Here they are, reprinted in all the magic of their top-notch, top-40 glory:

*Lyrics reprinted courtesy of Spencer FC, all rights reserved etc.*
WE'VE COME A LONG WAY
FROM THE HEADY DAYS

OF PLAYING FOOTBALL JUST USING OUR HANDS,

WE'VE BEEN A BIT AMBITIOUS,

WE'VE QUESTIONED OUR FITNESS,

BUT MINIMINTER AND THE SIDEMEN DON'T STAND A CHANCE,

WE'VE GOT OUR GAME PLAN DOWN,

AND NOW WE'RE HEADING TO THE PROMISED LAND.

*Chorus*

CAUSE WE'RE GOING ALL THE WAY,

ALL THE WAY TO WEMBLEY,

SPENCER FC FOR THE WEMBLEY CUP!

YEAH, WE'RE TAKING IT ALL THE WAY,

ALL THE WAY TO WEMBLEY

AND WE WON'T LEAVE TILL THE TROPHY'S OURS!

THE GAME'S FAST APPROACHING,

WE'VE DONE SOME FA COACHING,

WE GOT THE POWER PULSING THROUGH OUR VEINS,

SO WHEN YOU SEE US MARCH

OUT, UNDER THE LEGENDARY ARCH,

GET READY FOR THE GAME TO END ALL GAMES.

WE WILL ALL BE HEROES BY THE TIME IT COMES TO PLAY.

*Repeat chorus*

No football song would be complete without a rap, and Joe Weller and Vujanic invoked the spirit of John Barnes on New Order's 'World in Motion' for their section:

THE FAMOUS WEMBLEY IS WHERE WE'LL RAISE THE CUP,

CAPTAIN MINIMINTER GONNA SELF-DESTRUCT.

OUR TROOPS WILL BE RAPID, MOVE OUT THE WAY.

TOP SHOOTING SKILLS FROM MATT LE TISSIER.

SIDEMEN UNITED GONNA LOSE THE PLOT

WHEN THE F2 BOYS TIE THEM UP IN KNOTS.

BEEN DOWN THE GYM, WE'RE HARD AS STONE,

READY TO WIN WITH OUR MANAGER KEOWN.

YEAH, WE'RE TAKING IT ALL THE WAY

ALL THE WAY TO WEMBLEY

AND WE WON'T LEAVE TILL THE TROPHY'S OURS!

With the song settled and the team decided, there was only the small matter of the Wembley Cup final to be played.

When I envisaged the Wembley Cup final, I imagined a video as close to the *Match of the Day*-style and production values as possible. I wanted it to look every bit as professional as the BBC's FA Cup final coverage, and with the funds EE were providing along with a stroke of unbelievably good fortune, we were able to do just that.

Although we put the Wembley Cup final video up in August, we actually played the match a few months earlier, back in May. It was 31 May, to be precise – the day *after* the FA Cup final. What that meant was that we could have all of the gear they'd used to film that left in exactly the same place so we could use it for our match, and it would look just the same. We were going to produce something the like of which had never been seen on YouTube before.

I went to the FA Cup final that year to watch Arsenal thrash Aston Villa 4–0, and all I could think was, *In less than 24 hours I will be playing the biggest match of my life on this pitch.*

For an occasion like this, I wanted to prepare properly. I knew I wasn't the best player in that final, so I needed to do everything I could to maximise what ability I did have. I had a decent, healthy meal the night before and went to bed at a not unreasonable hour (or at least not unreasonable for a YouTuber organising the biggest event on his channel to date) at the hotel we were all staying at. The match was kicking off at 10am, and I wanted to feel ready.

I couldn't entirely control my nerves, however. I don't really get nervous before I play football, even in big games. It's usually just excitement for me – I can't wait to get out on the pitch and play. But on this occasion, perhaps because it was my baby, I was pretty nervous. I suddenly started worrying: after spending a year in the making of this show, what if none of the players turned up? What if it didn't go to plan? I struggled to sleep that night, but it turned out that I still got more rest than the Sidemen.

I think I've made it clear by now just how hard people on YouTube work, often staying up very late into the night to edit and make content because there just aren't enough hours in the day. So when you're talking about the Sidemen, some of the most successful and therefore busiest YouTubers around, you can begin to imagine the demands on their time.

Couple that with the Sidemen's notorious not-always-nocturnal sleeping patterns and it meant that a lot of the lads didn't make it to their hotel rooms until 6am ... which offered them the chance of about three hours' sleep before the big game.

You ask a professional footballer whether he'd fancy doing that the night before a cup final, and you'll hear a very unequivocal response!

Their lack of rest the night before the match certainly gave us a bit of a physical edge, but there had been some other concerns leading up to the game about how evenly matched the teams were.

When we originally planned the series, the idea was that MiniMinter and I would go head to head in a challenge in every episode, and whoever won would get first pick of a player, and whoever lost would take the next one, so that the winner of each challenge got the better player.

When the Sidemen calendar got so busy, we reinvented the concept so that the episodes were all about my team being built, with the Sidemen squad-building happening in the background. EE, understandably, wanted to make the most-watched series they possibly could. We all did. And to them that meant featuring the most popular YouTubers as much as possible.

To do that would mean having the F2 Freestylers on my team. Now, not every big YouTuber is necessarily a good football player, and even of those YouTubers who are pretty good, there's only a handful that can hold a candle to the F2 boys. Those guys were the best players in the group by far, and, what's more, they came as a package. They insisted that they played on the same team, and I could see their point. They were a double act, and you wouldn't break up the kind of chemistry that has seen them enjoy the success they have just to level the playing field.

Behind the scenes, I'd said all along that I was prepared not to have the F2 boys in my team (nothing personal, guys!).

I just knew it would look like I was getting all the best players. I always preferred the idea of being the underdog anyway. But it became increasingly clear that they had to be in my team so they could feature strongly in the series, which left us with what some would call mismatched teams, and understandably the Sidemen had some concerns.

We came to a solution that we thought would make everyone happy, but instead it made a certain group of people very unhappy in the comments under the video. We decided that we would take our tricky winger Manny, who is the brother of Sideman Tobi, and put him on the Sidemen team. We thought we'd be a bit creative and have a bit of fun with it.

On the day of the match, while we were all in the dressing room waiting to go out, there was no sign of Manny. And when I went to call him, there was a text message from him reading: 'Spencer, sorry but I was sent to spy on your team's prep ahead of the game. Had to keep it in the family and play with the Sidemen. No hard feelings bruv!'

Our team were, naturally, in uproar, and Joe Weller wound up his best WWE WrestleMania moves and kicked Manny's shirt to the ground, before Vujanic delivered an elbow drop to it.

Now, like WWE wrestling itself, there was a huge element of theatre to all of this, and I hold my hands up and admit that

I just did not anticipate how this would be taken. I assumed everyone would get what we were doing, just as they had on the FIFA Playa meets Spencer video, and that the viewers would have a certain amount of intuition about it. I thought they'd be in on the joke, and, to be fair, the majority of the audience probably got it. But sometimes it's easy to forget that some of the younger viewers don't have that intuition yet, and we should probably have seen what was coming.

Manny got caned in the comments, really harshly. People were calling him things like 'snake' for what he did to us, but he'd only been doing what we, the makers of the show, had asked him to do. We thought it would be quite funny and dramatic, and we weren't ready for that reaction. I certainly wouldn't have put Manny in that position if I'd known what was to come. I went on record in the days following the video release stating how good a sport he had been throughout it all and tried my best to defend him, but it was hard on Manny, who's a really decent guy. In the end it all blew over, thankfully. Manny got over it and he's smashing it on YouTube now.

That line between what's real and what's not had been regularly skated throughout the series. Of course, the episodes were scripted to a point (though the players' performance in the challenges were all their own), with things like the Sidemen's Ray Wilkins revelation planned in advance, and the Manny defection was another moment of that.

But once we're on the pitch and the whistle blows, everything is 100 per cent real. We play football, 11 against 11, and there is no script except for the one we write with our feet and our heads in the heat of the game.

The teams were, at least, a bit more even now, and with the two brothers now in their team the Sidemen had a potent double act of their own. RossiHD stepped up to take Manny's place in our team. Adding to the super-slick, *Match of the Day*-style production values, we had the perfect marriage of YouTube and professional football/BBC punditry in our presenters and commentary team. Taking our viewers through the day would be YouTuber True Geordie and former professional footballer Mark Bright, no stranger to Wembley Stadium. True Geordie, or Brian to call him by his real name, is a good pal of mine. We've done a lot together over the last few years and I have a lot of time for him. Like me, Brian is someone who'd already lived a very varied and interesting life before he came around to YouTube, and he's never short of a story on his very popular podcast. I personally think True Geordie's commentary made the Wembley Cup final what it was – he's made for the microphone. Mark wasn't bad either!

Their interview with the two managers, Ray Wilkins and Martin Keown, yielded some interesting insights. Martin Keown preached the value of keeping calm and moving the ball quickly, while Ray Wilkins's admission that he had 'a bunch of lunatics' on his side will have come as no surprise to anyone. He finished with some advice that we should 'enjoy the experience at Wembley because it will be their first and last time'.

We'll see about that, Ray!

With all of the preamble out of the way, it was finally time to kick off. Spencer FC vs Sidemen United in the first ever Wembley Cup.

• • •

It was quite a surreal experience, walking out to a stadium as big as Wembley with no crowd. The organisation for the stadium was very strict and we were only allowed a guest each, so my girlfriend didn't even get to see me stride out onto the Wembley turf as captain of Spencer FC. Besides, with all the editing work Alex was busy doing during that crazy year she probably wouldn't have been able to spare the time!

I gave my ticket to my mum, to return the favour for the spare ticket she gave me for Graham Norton's *Totally Saturday*. I didn't have any surprises in store for her, though, and I hoped the Sidemen wouldn't have any nasty surprises in store for our team either. My dad was there too, as physio for both teams, should things get a bit tasty. Anyone who's watched my channel for a while knows about the magic hands of Stevie CB!

My head was in two places as we lined up and then did the obligatory pre-match handshakes. On the one hand, I was thinking about the production and everything that went along with it, and on the other I was thinking, *I am about to play at Wembley Stadium*.

I needed to focus on the match if I was going to give a good account of myself, especially as it was undoubtedly going to be the biggest audience online ever to see me play. The thing I have always found about any game of football, at any level, is that, once the match starts, I just want to win. I'm desperate for it.

It would have been easy to get distracted by thoughts of the filming and how things would look onscreen later, but thankfully we had an absolutely amazing production team and that took a lot of the pressure off me. I was able to forget about the video for 90 minutes and just play a game of football – a game that just happened to be the biggest of my life so far.

We took our positions and I had to pinch myself as I adjusted my captain's armband on the Wembley turf. And then any such thoughts were immediately dispelled as the whistle blew and we were off. It was all about the game from now on.

It was a pretty tense start to the match, and Jeremy Lynch showed early on why his skills were in such high demand as he cut through the Sidemen defence, but it was MiniMinter's boys who had the first clear chance, with freestyler Daniel Cutting forcing Vujanic into action.

We drew first blood after five minutes, when Jeremy's pace helped him go clear and square an easy finish for RossiHD. What a way to announce your arrival in the team!

Sidemen United weren't about to give up the YouTube bragging rights without a fight, and Daniel Cutting scored a goal worthy of any cup final when he brought them level with a delicious chip over Vujanic. And if that wasn't enough, Cutting followed up with a cartwheel-and-somersault combo celebration every bit as delicious as the goal.

What do they say about the most likely time to concede a goal being straight after scoring one? Almost immediately afterwards, vice-captain Joe Weller burst through the middle and rifled a #SwiftReply, immediately justifying his demand to play centre-forward. And while his topless homage to Cristiano Ronaldo in celebration wasn't quite the equal of Daniel Cutting's somersault, it was definitely worthy of the obligatory yellow card for taking off his shirt.

Hugh Wizzy in the Sidemen goal had a couple of fraught moments, one when he was barged on the goal line and fumbled the ball (a foul was given), and another when he completely cleaned out Billy Wingrove à la Harald Schumacher at the 1982 World Cup semi-final. Billy was OK, though, so my dad rested easy on the sidelines with the stretcher.

Unbelievably, the referee allowed play to go on, and the Sidemen's very own freestyler made us pay. Daniel Cutting ran on to a great through ball and blasted it past Vujanic. Eighteen minutes had been played and it was already 2–2. It was breathless stuff.

The main difference I found between Wembley and any other ground I'd played on, aside from the faultless surface, was the size of the pitch. It felt huge, and playing at this breakneck speed meant that we were already feeling it. Steady on, lads, there's another 72 minutes to go here!

Manny's day wasn't about to get any better for him as he missed a sitter from a few yards out that should have put the Sidemen in front, and my dad was making himself busy by giving MiniMinter a quick shoulder massage on the sidelines. MiniMinter had been working till very late the night before so he probably needed a little stress reliever, but whose side are you on here, Dad?

We went in at half-time with the scores level, and Martin Keown shared some of his cup-final experience with us before we went out for the second. Daniel Cutting picked up where he had left off in the first half, hitting a sweet long-range effort that just went over.

We needed a reaction from the lads, and we got just that. In the 56th minute we put together a slick move with the F2 Freestylers at the heart of it. RossiHD, real name Ryan, who had been wrongly pulled up for offside only minutes before, was lurking once again, and he put us in front with another straightforward finish. We couldn't let our lead slip again, could we?

It was all Spencer FC now. Sidemen United keeper Hugh Wizzy made amends for some of his more eccentric moments in the first half with a top-drawer save from a Billy rocket, but in the 65th minute ChrisMD made it 4–2 and that was surely game over.

It certainly felt that way when Wroetoshaw scored a perfectly good goal for the Sidemen that was disallowed. Video replays afterwards showed that it had crossed the line, and there were shades of Frank Lampard's shot for England against Germany at the World Cup in 2010. During the game I had no idea whether it had crossed the line or not so there's nothing you can do but play to the whistle. We definitely had luck on our side there though!

Fairly early on in the game I'd moved back to centre-back to help shore up the defence, and I was shattered as the match reached its later stages after covering so much extra ground on the huge Wembley pitch. I was starting to get cramp. I wasn't the only one struggling either. There were some tired Sidemen

United legs and not much defensive fight left as Billy sealed a 5–2 victory for us. It probably flattered us, but I wasn't about to complain.

When the whistle blew, it was a great feeling … but I'm not sure I entirely allowed myself to enjoy it fully. Just as the switch had been flicked in my mind when we kicked off, which meant game time, so the final whistle flicked that switch again so that I was now thinking about the video, and mulling over the ramifications of the result. Oh, yes, and I was catching my breath too!

Victory for Spencer FC was a great result for me and my channel. You couldn't have written a better script for it, really, though people have asked me since, 'What would you have done if you'd lost?'

If we'd lost we'd have lost, simple as that. We'd have said we wanted to be back next year to have another go at it. The action on the pitch was 100 per cent real, so the outcome was out of my control. But what a result!

That first Wembley Cup was an absolute gamechanger for me. The smartest thing I got out of the deal with EE wasn't money, but the right to have the content on my channel rather than an EE-branded channel. That content was easily the biggest in terms of views so far on my channel, with the final eventually attracting over 16 million viewers.

Having the Wembley Cup content on my channel and the support of all the other YouTube lads playing gave me a massive injection of hundreds of thousands of new subscribers, so that every video I made after that got substantially more views than before. In the long term, that would mean more money in the form of advertising revenue, which is earned according to the amount of views. Money that I could then plough back in to making content of a similar quality. I think in total my channel grew by more than 250,000 subscribers during the few weeks that the Wembley Cup content was released. Insane.

My first appearance at Wembley was a dream come true for my channel. It really put me on the map and opened doors in ways I was yet to fully appreciate. On a personal level, I loved playing there, but it didn't really sink in at the time as my mind was in two places at once, both on the production and the match itself. It was only later that I thought to myself, *Bloody hell, I played at Wembley!*

I'd come a long way from the guy sitting in his bedroom editing videos at 3am while his girlfriend slept in the bed next to him, and I made a promise to myself that, if I was lucky enough to get to play at the home of football a second time, I'd try to appreciate the moment just that little bit more.

# HALF-TIME: THIS IS WHERE THE MAGIC HAPPENS

# 7

# HASHTAG IT!

I came out of the Wembley Cup on a high unlike any I'd experienced before. I was really happy with the content we'd made, my subscriber numbers had rocketed and my only thought was, *I want to do this all the time*.

Playing at Wembley obviously wasn't something I could do every week – but playing football on my channel was very much within my grasp. For whatever reason, people seemed to love watching YouTubers playing football. We weren't the best players around by a long way, but there was something that was making people tune in.

The idea of starting my own football club began to take shape (I told you I'd always wanted to own one), and my channel was now making me enough income that I could afford to plough that money back into it and fund my own football content.

Of course, that didn't mean I could afford to pay the biggest YouTubers to play every week. And, on top of that, the logistical difficulties of coordinating the diaries of these guys was a headache even for a one-off match, much less a weekly game. No, if I was going to do it on a regular basis it would have to be with a group of people who weren't YouTubers. Now, who did I know who was pretty decent at football and would be up for playing on YouTube every week? Let me see ...

Hashtag United existed as a team long before it made its debut on YouTube. Faisal Manji and I started it as a seven-a-side team when we were both living in Clapham, south London, and we played every Sunday in a league. My friends Woody, TJ and Lovatt – all boys who had also played for Carmichael-Browns Athletic (CBA) when we were at school – played in the team too. However, just as a lot of people stop playing football when they turn 16 and their youth team finishes, so a lot of people hit their mid to late twenties and stop too. People start having children, getting married and become busier in their careers, and adult reality starts to bite. There just isn't as much time for football any more.

I definitely hit such a period. After moving to Hertfordshire I had to temporarily hang up my Hashtag boots, although

Woody and Faisal kept the team going in London in my absence. During that mad year of work with Alex, I was playing once a week for Taplow Swans, where a load of my mates still played, but then we moved back to Essex and that stopped. If you'd asked me then if I thought it was likely I'd be playing regular 11-a-side football again, I'd have said no. I was too busy with work and just couldn't see it happening.

I definitely didn't want to take my foot off the YouTube gas, but what if I could create the perfect marriage between producing content for my channel and playing football regularly? What could be better than that? To do it with my mates too, and keep together that group of players with the history we had with each other, well, that would be pretty special too, wouldn't it?

The plan all along was to make more football content on my channel. I just never thought it would be content of me actually playing football, much less in the team I had been part of on and off for the best part of a decade.

Hashtag's beginnings, however, were rooted in some devastating news.

September 2015 marked the third anniversary of the death of a friend of mine from school. Joe Surtees had played for CBA when we were at sixth form together. He was a very fit and healthy guy who out of nowhere suddenly got leukaemia.

I visited him in hospital a few times when he was ill, which was while I was working for Copa90, and I thought he was recovering well. And then I got a phone call from Faisal one day at work saying that Joe had died. It was awful news and a real wake-up call: a reminder of just how precious our time on this planet is and how quickly it can be taken away from us.

We decided to put on a memorial match in honour of Joe, with all the lads from the old CBA team taking on Joe's university mates. We made a prize, the Joe Surtees Memorial Trophy, and I planned to put on a whole day of it and film the occasion.

A couple of days before the game, we learned that another member of that CBA team, Daniel Chalangary, our goalkeeper, had passed away too. We had lost two of our school team already and we were only in our mid-twenties.

We wanted the day to be a celebration of the two guys, and it was a great afternoon and we raised a good bit of money for a blood-cancer charity. We, CBA, won the match on penalties, and I did some commentary over the highlights of the game. I'd never put a football match I'd played in up on my channel before (with the exception of the Wembley Cup), and I thought it was a good way to introduce my viewers to my mates.

A lot of people in the comments said they'd love to see us play again, and then a YouTube channel called The Football

Republic, where my younger brother Saunders used to work, saw the video and offered us the perfect opportunity.

In the spirit of that number-one YouTube rule for growth, collaboration, The Football Republic challenged us to a match. This game offered us the perfect chance to see if we still had what it takes and it would produce what eventually became a pilot episode of our brand-new football series that ended up being a huge part of the channel.

If we were going to do this, we needed to do it right. I had no desire to just sit someone at the side of the pitch with a camera and see what they could film. I wanted to recapture some of the production values that had made the Wembley Cup so successful. For me, if this was going to work it would need to represent the same thing the Wembley Cup did – a load of mates getting to do stuff that your normal amateur footballer doesn't get to. That included having high-quality footage of every game so that we could relive all the best (and worst) bits afterwards. I wanted it to be filmed with multiple cameras, so we needed to get all the gear necessary for that, and we got some football kits sorted with the Spencer FC badge on them.

Of course, one thing we did need to do was put the actual team together. The original Hashtag United was a seven-a-side team, so we needed to pull in some extra players to make up the numbers. Naturally, I turned to my brother Seb, and he brought some of his mates from school and university into the fold. I knew many of them very well – some of them through a slightly bizarre way.

When we were younger, Seb and I created custom teams with our mates on *Pro Evolution Soccer*, and we'd battle it out on a regular basis. My team was made up of the CBA lads and Seb, being at university at the time, based his around his University of Northampton First XI team. Through this I learned of players like Dan Brown, Phil Martin, John Dawson and Andy Jeffs-Watts long before I had the pleasure of meeting them in real life.

I got us a manager for the match too, the absolute legend that is Adebayo 'The Beast' Akinfenwa.

Now, I had no idea how we were going to get on in the game – it was all a bit of an experiment, really. Would we get thrashed? If we did, would that dim my enthusiasm for it? Was there any real appetite for amateur football with my mates instead of star-draw YouTubers?

We were about to find out if this idea had legs.

The Football Republic were managed by True Geordie, who had commentated on the Wembley Cup, and there would be two matches, one played on my channel and another on theirs. I needn't have had any fears about whether we'd get thrashed. After Akinfenwa demanded some pure 'Beast mode' from us, we did just that and ran out 3–0 winners on my channel, before we dished out an even more convincing 7–1 thrashing on theirs.

Seb's mates took us up a level, no doubt about it. We already had some good players in my group, but lads like Phil Martin and Dan Brown were pure class. I came off the pitch thinking we didn't look too bad at all. We'd also inadvertently created one of the best strike partnerships I've ever played with – Dan Brown and Ryan Adams. Ryan was my mate from Taplow Swans, and teaming up with Dan Brown, a player nearly a decade older than him, was a match made in heaven.

But, as ever on YouTube, it was up to the viewers to decide. At the end of the video on my channel, I asked if people would like us to keep the team together and do it regularly. The response was overwhelming, with 99 per cent of people wanting us to do it. Unlike the time I solicited advice on whether I should continue working with Vincent Kompany, I went with the 99 per cent.

By this stage, Seb had officially joined Alex and me on the business side of things. He'd always been my go-to person for advice, so when things really started taking off it made sense for him to actually take on the commercial side of the channel. I hadn't seen much of him when we'd lived in Hertfordshire at the same time, but I would be seeing a lot more of him now.

We put our heads together and started asking ourselves, 'What does this football-club series we want to do look like? What is this team? What are we even going to call it?'

I didn't want to call the team Spencer FC in the long term. I'd always cringed at the fact that some people had thought I'd called our youth team Carmichael-Browns Athletic after myself, rather than as a bit of publicity for my dad's company in return for money for our kit. This wasn't about making it the Spencer show – I wanted it to exist as a separate entity, like a new brand. Something that we felt, done properly, would have potential to grow a lot bigger than little old me.

I know that I can't play football for ever. Making the club separate to Spencer FC would allow it to continue after I'd hung up my boots, and it would mean it could be something everyone in the team could take seriously and believe in. And that, after all, was what this team was about: a group of people with a shared history making something new to continue playing together – and to explore the limits of what was possible as a YouTube football club.

With our past in mind, there could only be one name: Hashtag United. It was perfect. We made a new YouTube channel and other social-media accounts for Hashtag United (though the videos would go on Spencer FC as well), and we designed what I think is a pretty decent badge too.

The trolls like to say things like, 'Why are you named after a keyboard button? What does it even mean?' But the simple fact is that it is a very modern symbol and word that is known almost exclusively from its use in social media. As we are a club that represents a new wave of football, born of social-media and online platforms, the hashtag encapsulates this perfectly. You can use the # symbol as shorthand for the club – #. You can play around with it on social media. You can even make the symbol with your hands, something we've not been shy about doing since we formed.

Next, we needed a concept. I was adamant that we wouldn't be just another Sunday league team. Quite a few people were doing Sunday league on YouTube already, and years before Spencer FC, I'd done something similar with the semi-pro team my dad was a physio with, East Thurrock United.

I started filming their games and the team talks, and putting together a little highlights reel with me commentating over it. It was pretty straightforward, and I definitely hadn't found my YouTube persona yet, but I got some great footage. It was proper aggressive stuff at this level. The manager would go mad at the players in the dressing room, swearing his head off and letting it all out like one of those fly-on-the-wall documentaries about football clubs. Think *The Four Year Plan* (about QPR) or *Being: Liverpool*, but at a much lower level.

The non-league side of football is something I'm quite passionate about and I've travelled with East Thurrock to many a game, including their first-round FA Cup tie against Hartlepool and their eventual promotion to the National League South. There was a time when Seb and I thought Hashtag should be a semi-pro team from the off, one that we didn't play in but instead the series would be about us running the club and trying to gain promotion to professional football. However, we felt that this was an opportunity we could revisit at a later date. There was a timeframe on how long we could continue to play football ourselves and, for whatever reason, our audience seemed to want to see us play, so we decided to concentrate on that before it was too late.

So I felt that Sunday league content had been done, and on top of that, there were limitations around it that would have severely interfered with my plans. Firstly, in Sunday league you're playing in a league system with loads of random people. They might not want to be filmed. On top of that, you're then going to monetise that content. You would need release forms to cover you, otherwise you might find yourself on extremely dodgy ground.

I never want to build something on a base that could be pulled away from me. The business side of YouTube is one that the comments section and viewers don't always appreciate, but there are a lot of content creators out there who build channels and careers off what is essentially illegal content. It wasn't something I was prepared to do. Imagine if we won a huge cup final but then the opposition refused to sign release forms and we couldn't legally upload the content from it? No, if we were going to do this we'd need to know that our hard work and results, good or bad, would be there to stay for the audience.

The second concern was the venues. In my post-Wembley Cup world I wanted high production values, which meant filming the matches in a very specific way. You need to film football from high up to make it look decent, and you can't do that on a Hackney Marshes pitch. On top of that, games get called off all the time – waterlogged pitches, the other team not being able to field a side, you name it. If I wanted to build a series on YouTube that my viewers could rely on, I didn't want to have to say, 'Sorry, we've got no video for the next three weeks because the weather's been terrible.'

So we decided to take all these limitations around Sunday league off the table and protect ourselves a bit. We found ourselves a 3G pitch – a synthetic surface – so that we'd never have to call a game off because of the weather. This pitch was in a stadium in north London, which meant we could mount our cameras high to make the games look decent.

I think some people on YouTube might have got a bit confused by what we were doing, almost as if we thought we were too good for Sunday league. Nothing could be further from the truth. We'd all played Sunday league football for a decade and some of us still do. Playing for Taplow Swans had been my big release at the end of a tough week and I loved it. We all loved Sunday league. The question wasn't 'Do we like Sunday league?' It was 'Do we want to build a series around Sunday league?'

The answer was no. But without the Sunday league structure, what would we do?

Before we'd even sorted the minor detail of the format of the league system we'd compete in, we managed to land ourselves a kit and sponsorship deal.

We did a deal with Umbro where we would have our own bespoke kits made by them to the same standards of a top-flight club's, and in the meantime we would wear a yellow-and-blue off-the-peg kit with our badge on. Loads of teams on YouTube wear a kit made by a well-known sports brand, but we were the first to do a proper deal with one and have an official kit provider. This meant we were an approved reseller of Umbro too and were legally allowed to sell their merchandise. This was a big moment for me. Umbro had made the England kit throughout my entire childhood, and now me and my mates had a proper deal with them on our own team's kit. Insane!

To my mind, football kits look weird without a sponsor or at least something in the middle of the jersey. Even Barcelona, who had famously gone without a shirt sponsor for years, eventually came round to this way of thinking. Thankfully, EE, who we'd worked with so well on the Wembley Cup, were able to offer us a short-term deal. They were happy with the exposure, and we were happy with a good-looking kit complete with a sponsor.

It was on the train to talk to Umbro about the kit that we finally nailed the concept of the series, too. Seb and I were going back and forth, and then he said, 'Why don't we do it like a *Road to Glory* series on *FIFA*?'

I'd made loads of these *Road to Glory* series on my channel, in which you start off in Division 10, obviously playing other people in Division 10 (which usually means they aren't much good), and work your way up to Division 1. You have to get a certain amount of points within 10 games to get promoted. It starts off easy in Division 10, with only 12 points required for promotion, but then gets progressively more demanding as you climb the pyramid, with 23 points from 10 games required to win the title in Division 1.

You might play other people in these matches, but you're not in a league against them. The only person you're in a league with is yourself. You're completely siloed off in that regard. That's brilliant on *FIFA*, because it means you're not stuck in a league structure where you're waiting for other people to play. You can log on at any time of the day or night and find someone in the world to play you.

And that's where it became appealing for us. It meant we had the freedom to know we could always have a game, and because we would only be in a league against ourselves, it meant every episode would simply feature our matches.

It was a brilliant idea from Seb, and it was an idea that was completely applicable to my audience. They loved *FIFA* and seemed to enjoy my *Road to Glory* videos, and they would totally get this. It might take a bit of explaining to someone outside the *FIFA* YouTube community – 'So who else is in this division?' But that was OK by us. This was a new form of football, after all.

We decided on a five-division structure instead of ten, with the idea that we would play a match every couple of weeks all year round (with no summer break, unlike those work-shy types in the pro leagues!). We had no way of knowing how long it would take us to work through the divisions because we didn't really have any idea how good we were, but I was quietly confident that we could probably get the job done in a couple of years, which seemed like a good amount of time.

I wanted to make a big commitment to something, but I didn't want to get stuck languishing in Division 5 indefinitely.

We had a couple of guys in their mid-thirties, and I couldn't be sure how long they would want to continue playing, so two years seemed to make sense. Besides, I couldn't guarantee the show would be popular, either, so if we made it to two years I'd know we'd be doing something right. What we'd do after we won the Division 1 title, if we ever did at all, we didn't know yet, but we figured we'd cross that bridge when we came to it.

One thing we were sure about was that we didn't want to go out challenging the best teams in the area and get smashed every time from day one. In *FIFA*, when you start out in Division 10, you play easier teams and it's pretty straightforward to get promoted. So we wanted things to mirror the *FIFA* game and give us an opportunity to get used to playing together again, otherwise we risked getting smashed in Division 5 and killing the series before it even started.

To do this, we decided to theme the divisions, and so for Division 5 we picked a theme that would give us the best chance of winning some games. The theme was other YouTube channels (sorry, guys – no disrespect intended!), and we'd work our way up to the bigger challenges as we hopefully climbed the divisions.

I'd always dreamed of owning a football club, but I'd thought that was an ambition I was years away from. But here we were, making one. With the kit, the stadium, the team and the format in place, there was just one thing left to do: play some football.

• • •

Hashtag United's first official game in Division 5 was against Dream Team FC ... plus a very special ringer they had in their line-up.

Filming inside the dressing room for the videos I made for my dad's team, East Thurrock, was in my mind as I made this a big part of the Hashtag episodes. In the first video, we get our brand-new, box-fresh kit from Umbro, complete with names and squad numbers on the back of the shirts.

It wasn't the only idea I took from my East Thurrock days. I had made my dad the physio, drawing another nice little line from our beginnings as CBA. And I would commentate over each video, offering unbiased[4] insights into the match.

I gave a little pre-match team talk and announced the starting line-up – without the expletives from the manager that coloured the East Thurrock videos – before I told the boys that 'The Chairman' was offering us an incentive to win our first game: a brand-new pair of Umbro boots of our choosing. The rewards offered by our mysterious Chairman

---

[4]  Well, maybe not *entirely* unbiased, but I do try!

would become a regular feature of the series, and this was once again an example of us borrowing a mechanism from video games, as we saw these challenges as accomplishments like you may find on Xbox or PlayStation. As for who the Chairman was, that's a whole different matter entirely ...

This being YouTube, the matches were collaborations, so often we would have a rematch on our opponent's channel afterwards to give them some content to take from the game. These rematches were more like friendlies. They wouldn't affect our standing in the division – only the match on my channel would do that.

Now, let's Hashtag it, boys! We kicked off against Dream Team FC, and we could see a very special player in their line-up. Cherno Samba is an ex-professional footballer you might not have heard of ... unless you've played *Football Manager*, that is. He is a *Football Manager* legend, an absolute world beater in the computer game, and it was a nice touch to have him on the field with us.

His *Football Manager* stats couldn't help his team here, though, and fittingly it was Faisal Manji, one of the original people behind the Hashtag seven-a-side team and CBA, who scored Hashtag United's first goal proper in its new guise.

We went on to win the game 3–2, an amazing result in our first match, and we secured both the Umbro boots, thanks to the Chairman, and, most importantly, the three points. We needed 12 points from 10 games to get promoted (though there would be no dead rubbers: if we secured the 12 points quicker than that, we would be instantly promoted). Getting three in our first match was a great start.

Next up, we played my old mates at Copa90. In my pre-match talk I explained to the lads that the Chairman, who only ever really seemed to speak to me, had promised us something really special if we got three points: a game at Wembley Stadium. Maybe I would get a second chance there after all, Mr Ray Wilkins! The lads were thrilled at the possibility, particularly Seb, who I know would have loved to have played in the 2015 Wembley Cup.

We'd had a really good camera set-up in the first match, using the height that a stadium afforded us, a four-man crew and six cameras including GoPros in each goal to offer some decent video replays. But we took things up a notch in this game with some broadcast-television-quality graphics of the team sheet, made by YouTube *FIFA* royalty Marius Hjerpseth, laid out in formation. It was pretty slick stuff, and our *en vogue* 4–2–3–1 formation, with Dan 'not *The Da Vinci Code* author' Brown at the tip of it, wasn't too bad either.

We listed the substitutes in the graphics, as well as the man playing in that all-important behind-the-camera role, my younger brother Saunders. Hashtag was becoming a real family affair, with both of my brothers and my dad involved, and Saunders, despite not playing on the pitch, was every bit as vital to the operation as anyone in the team.

Saunders directs the Hashtag shoots, and he and a couple of mates he lives with, Glen and Robbie, basically have a production company going in their house. They edit the Hashtag games for us, and then I add my voiceover and give them a quick once-over before they go up. It was great to have someone I could not only trust, but who had all the right skills necessary for the production. Saunders had been professionally trained as a cameraman and editor and was already flourishing in the industry off his own bat, having worked for FremantleMedia and done plenty of YouTube content for them. He has his own YouTube channel as well called Saunders Says, where he does travel and lifestyle vlogging. I highly recommend it!

Copa90 had some familiar faces in their team in the form of my Wembley Cup teammates Poet and Vujanic, and it was great to see them, but once the whistle blew it was all business. It was a tight match, but that man Dan Brown justified his first start for Hashtag United by opening the scoring, and Ryan 'not the American singer-songwriter and definitely not the ageing Canadian rocker called Bryan' Adams got us a second. They would become two very familiar names on our scoresheet. Despite Copa90 getting a goal back, we were good for a 2–1 win ... and a trip to Wembley.

Playing at Wembley with my fellow YouTubers had been fantastic, the best football experience of my life so far, but doing it with my mates – this was next level. I went way back with these Hashtag boys. Faisal and I had kicked a ball about in the Hatfield Peverel train station car park together when we were kids who couldn't find anywhere else to play, and now we were playing at Wembley. That's pinch-yourself stuff. As a group, we had football history, friendship history and family history. There quite simply was no group of lads I'd rather be doing this with. But we weren't there to make up the numbers: I knew from experience that you enjoy these occasions all the more when you leave with a victory.

Our opponents were Vauxhall, one of the England football team sponsors, and they'd taken a leaf out of Dream Team's book and got themselves a couple of ringers. Former England internationals Ray Parlour and Graeme Le Saux would be turning out for them.

I was determined to savour the moment a bit more this time, and we even did the national anthem, which was special. Typically, as soon as the whistle went, all I could concentrate on was winning. And, boy, did we win that day.

We were 4–0 up after half an hour, and Ray Parlour was going mental. He started kicking off. 'Who on earth made these teams?' he shouted, and all I could do was think, *What are you on about – you've got you and Graeme Le Saux on your team!*

Those guys couldn't influence the game though, perhaps because for them this was just another game at Wembley following an illustrious career made up of games a million times more important than this, and we ran out 8–2 winners. For us, this was as big as it got, so we made sure to leave it all on the pitch. Three games in, a 100 per cent record, and to play and win our third game at Wembley ... to do that with my mates was something beyond my wildest dreams. And not just mine.

Rich Beck is one of my best mates from uni. I played alongside him in his dad's Taplow Swans Sunday league side, and he was now Hashtag's 'man-mountain' (the name given to him by Akinfenwa in our pilot-episode game) centre-back. He scored two penalties that day, and he told me later that it was his life's goal to score at Wembley. It was just amazing and empowering to think we were really making all of our dreams come true, together.

And it didn't stop there. The next match would offer a chance to make one of my teenage self's greatest ambitions come true when we took on the people behind the reason I spent so much of my adolescence locked away in my bedroom: the makers of *Football Manager*.

These guys weren't just a bunch of armchair football fans. They had a really decent five-a-side team who I'd come up against before, and I knew that we would get turned over if we weren't at our best, so I really drilled into the guys just how important this game was. If we won, we were promoted to Division 4, so there was a lot on the line.

As if that wasn't enough, the Chairman had negotiated an amazing incentive for a Hashtag victory. If we beat the *Football Manager* team, we would be put into the actual game of *Football Manager 2017* as 'newgens'. Now, for those of you who don't play *Football Manager*, what that means is that, when you go through the game for a good few seasons and the current crop of players get old and retire, new youth-team players come through to be the stars of tomorrow. In among those new players would be us: there'd be a Spencer Owen, a Ryan Adams, a Rich Beck. Hats off to the Chairman – it was a hell of an incentive.

I privately thought we might get turned over in that game, having seen their five-a-side team, but instead we smashed them 7–1 – an incredible result for us. We had been promoted in the minimum amount of time possible, and as the cries of '*Championes, championes, olé, olé, olé!*' went out in the dressing room afterwards, I allowed myself a little moment.

As a teenager I'd dreamed about being in *Football Manager*, even though I'd got into football late and becoming a pro was never an option for me anyway. How else would you feature in the game unless you were a professional footballer?

We were rewriting the rule book. I wasn't even the best player at school, and yet I'd made it into the game. I'd done it my own way, outside of the traditional channels, and we were just getting started.

· · ·

In Division 4 we would need 15 points for promotion. We upped the difficulty level, just like you would in *FIFA*, and we started playing some harder teams as we changed the theme to 'staff teams'. We went straight in at the deep end in our first match, as we took on Manchester City's staff, a team made up of some social-media and coaching staff and one or two surprise packages.

To make things trickier still, we were leaving the familiar surroundings of our 3G stadium behind to play at Man City's incredibly impressive training facilities next to the Etihad Stadium. This was technically our first away game (Wembley is more like a cup final).

If you work at a football club it usually means you're pretty decent at football. Added to that, Man City's staff were able to call upon the services of some ex-pros, and their former striker Paul Dickov captained the side. They were the hardest team we had played so far, and Dickov scored from 40 yards out with an outrageous goal. It was just ridiculous. But we fought back well to draw the game 3–3, and a draw was an excellent away point against a very good team.

Things didn't get any easier in the next game, which was a bit of an emotional one for my family. We would be taking on Umbro's staff team at Upton Park, home of West Ham United, the team we all went to watch together every week now we had season tickets. This was the summer of 2016, and West Ham had already played their last game at the ground, which was an emotional occasion in itself. Saunders, Seb, my dad and I were all there to see them come from behind to beat Manchester United 3–2 in an epic encounter. The club were moving to their new home at the Olympic Stadium the following season.

Unbelievably, this wasn't the first time I'd be playing at Upton Park. In fact, I'd played there just a few weeks before in front of 20,000 people, as part of an England Legends XI side that played a German Legends side on the 50th anniversary of the 1966 World Cup final. I wasn't one of the legends, of course – they made up the starting XI – but I joined a group of non-professional footballers (such as actor Damian Lewis from *Homeland* and *Billions*, and comedians Jack Whitehall and Russell Howard) on the bench.

The Germans have never been famous for their sense of humour, so their bench was packed with ex-pros, including Oliver Neuville. Our manager was actor Ray Winstone, while former German international Michael Ballack led the Germans. That should tell you something about how seriously the respective teams were taking it.

Having said all that, I was still ticking another lifelong dream off the bucket list. Playing for England in any form was not to be taken lightly, and lining up to sing the national anthem in front of the Upton Park crowd was an amazing moment for me.

I came on in the second half when we were already 5–0 down. The sight of me and a couple of comedians coming on didn't exactly strike fear into the hearts of the Germans, but I did have one pretty cool moment. When Oliver Neuville raced clear, perhaps a shade slower than he might have been in his prime, I managed to get back and tackle him. This was my first time playing in front of a proper crowd, and because the West Ham fans knew I was a supporter of the club too, they gave me a big cheer for that one. Adding to that, I played alongside ex-West Ham players such as David James and Rio Ferdinand, which made for an unbelievable experience!

Apart from the result, of course. The Germans won 7–2 and they were clearly taking it seriously as an opportunity for revenge, especially when you consider that the guy who got both of our goals wasn't even a footballer. It was former England rugby player Ben Cohen.

I was hoping for a very different result with the Hashtag boys against Umbro at Upton Park, and I knew that both sides would be taking it very seriously indeed. There was still room for a little sentiment, however – this would be my last memory of this stadium, after all – as Saunders came out from behind the camera to get his Hashtag kit on and take his place on the bench. He was joined by a familiar face in the form of Wembley Cup player Manny, a welcome addition to any team.

Umbro had *TOWIE* star Mark Wright, who was a semi-pro player, and his brother Josh, who is a current professional player for Gillingham, in their ranks, so they looked decent. They also had a striker who looked to be about 7ft tall, which would pose its own problems.

We came out on top 3–2 in a very close game, and Saunders came on in the second half before we made a substitution no one was expecting: my dad came on so that all four of us, who had enjoyed so many amazing memories at this ground watching West Ham play, could have one final memory to enjoy. #livingthedream – seriously!

Our next match was no joke – or at least it wasn't supposed to be – as I finally put those years spent doing stand-up comedy to good use by asking some comedians to put together a team. People like Jack Whitehall and Russell Howard are decent players – Russell's unbelievable, actually – and I thought they'd provide a stern test for us.

Russell Howard didn't play, however, and as for Jack Whitehall . . .

The night before the match Alex and I were at Glastonbury Festival, watching Adele headline the Pyramid Stage before we headed home on the long drive so I could get back in time for our game. Jack was there, and I was chatting away to him. When Alex and I got ready to leave, I asked him if he was coming back for the game and he just looked at me and grinned. 'I'm not going to make it, mate,' he said. He was having a good time and had no intention of leaving Glastonbury on account of a football match!

It was probably a good call by him, to be honest. We took on a load of his comedian buddies but the real punchline in the end was the result. We won 19–1, despite the comedians calling upon the services of former professional footballer Lee Hendrie. They were so bad, in fact, that even I managed to score. My first ever goal for Hashtag United! Ryan Adams registered the first hat-trick – or hash-trick, as we called it – for the team, and Dan Brown wasn't far behind with his. In the end they scored five goals each that game.

We got a bit of stick for that match in the comments section, saying things like, 'Oh, you guys are just playing rubbish teams on purpose.' But that simply wasn't the case. We'd played some really good sides like Manchester City and Umbro, and it was also a bit of a learning curve for us. We just didn't know what level we were capable of – but we were having a great time finding out.

The comedians match was the first game with our new goalkeeper, Andy Jeffs-Watts. Our previous goalkeeper, Dan

Pheysey, had decided to step down after the Umbro game. Dan works for YouTube, which is how I got to know him, and he's a good mate. He was getting quite a bit of stick in the comments for some of his performances, particularly after Paul Dickov's 40-yard screamer.

Dan has a pretty thick skin and could handle the criticism, but in the end an opportunity to go and work abroad combined with the harshness of the comments meant he opted to step down. We were sad to see him leave but we were able to pull in a top-class replacement. Andy Jeffs-Watts was Seb's old university-team goalkeeper.

The YouTube comments can be incredibly cruel, as anyone in this industry knows. I always tell the Hashtag boys to take them with a pinch of salt. Don't get me wrong, often there's some really valuable feedback and insight left in the comments section, but the fact is that there is so much vile nonsense left by keyboard warriors who just want to watch the world burn it means sometimes it's not worth reading them.

The benefit of doing what we do on YouTube is that every time you score a great goal, it's captured on video. You can watch it back whenever you want to, and a million people will see it and think you're a hero.

The flipside, of course, is that for every howler you make, you're going to get stick in the comments. Trolls are just part and parcel of the internet, and you have to be able to deal with that.

It is different for goalkeepers, though. They have it tough at any level: they only have to make one mistake and it's a goal and they get hammered for it, whereas I could get away with all sorts of mistakes in the middle of the park and there wouldn't always be such severe repercussions. Except the odd troll telling me I'm the worst player in the team, of course. They might have a point, though ...

Dan Pheysey would be missed, but given that he's now living the life out in LA and smashing it, I think he's got over the experience.

We won games against a very good Google staff team and then YouTube channel Ball Street, before we took on the West Ham United staff team. We hadn't lost a game so far as Hashtag United – our only draw had come against the Manchester City team – and a win here would see us promoted to Division 3.

Now, when we started playing Hashtag games there was definitely the sense that we cared more about the result than the opposition. We had a league structure and rewards on the line, so we had some great incentives to win, whereas for our opponents the games were little more than friendlies, with an opportunity for content for their YouTube channels if they had one.

This meant that we beat some teams we had no right to beat, really, teams with ex-pros in them, and even an Umbro side with a current professional footballer in their ranks, all because we were more up for it than the opposition.

However, as we played more games, our opponents became increasingly aware that there were up to a million people watching these matches on YouTube, and that they'd better start wanting it a bit more if they were to avoid losing face on the internet.

West Ham had cottoned on and most definitely did not want to get mugged off in front of a big online audience, so they decided to tool up with some serious players in their 'staff' team. They brought a few lads from their academy and some players recently released by their academy – so still brilliant footballers, in other words – and maybe a couple of members of staff.

I just thought, *Are you kidding me?* In many ways it was a mark of respect, but at the time that's not what's going through your head.

If I'm honest, I'd have to say I would rather play a team with some ex-pros in than a bunch of hungry, fit-as-a-fiddle young lads who play week in, week out with each other. The young players just want it more. And so it proved as we lost our first game, going down 2–0 to a bunch of very good players indeed. We would not be going up to Division 3 just yet.

From a football point of view, I hated it. I always hate losing, no matter what the situation, but from a creative point of view – looking at it as the person running a YouTube channel – defeat was good for us. We were getting a fair bit of stick by now for either not playing good enough teams – which was just nonsense in my book, as we were working really hard for our wins – or, as some people even accused us of, fixing the games, which was just plain offensive. A strong reminder of the ridiculousness of YouTube comments.

Anyone who knows me would absolutely back me up in saying that there is no way I would ever want to be part of something like that. Some people have even suggested that we're paying the refs, and my answer is, 'Well, someone has to – they're not going to do it for free!'

The games are the games – once the whistle goes they are 100 per cent real. The referees are impartial, just as they should be in any league at any level, but especially one in which a million people are watching the matches. Many of the refs we use are commonly officiating at a decent standard too, be it the Ryman League or other semi-professional levels.

We do, however, create drama around the match, just like we did with Manny changing sides in the Wembley Cup. We will do that outside of the match because we're also creating a piece of entertainment, something that I hope sets us apart slightly from the other matches being put out on YouTube channels.

But even some of that drama is grounded in reality. As captain of the side, I deliver pre-match, half-time and post-match talks, which are filmed for the show. The reason we do it is so we can explain to the viewers who our opponents are, what potential rewards might be up for grabs and what it means to our progress in the division. These aren't really scripted, however, as much of what I talk about, particularly at half-time, is a reaction to the match we're playing.

But even if the cameras weren't there, I would still have a chat with the lads at these points during a match. When you're playing football for real, you don't say, 'Right, lads, let me do my five-minute speech now, please.' But everyone will say their bit, including me, and for some games you don't need to do one: everyone knows their jobs, there's nothing to say so let's just go and play.

We secured promotion in our next game, winning 7–2 against another YouTube channel, 1080 Football. We enjoyed the moment, but the accusations of having it all too easy weren't going to go away in a hurry with a scoreline like that, no matter how unfair that was on the 1080 Football lads.

Perversely, we needed to lose more games.

One stream of comments just wouldn't go away. We were constantly being told that we would get smashed by a team called Palmers FC, a Sunday league side with a decent YouTube presence.

Some ill-informed viewers thought that because we weren't playing in a Sunday league we were somehow inferior to Sunday league teams. I've had the pleasure of playing with many different amateur teams in many different Sunday league set-ups over the past decade, and I can honestly say Hashtag United would destroy every single one of them. We have something special. There are zero barriers to entry to play in Sunday league, anyone can do it. How teams who played at that level were somehow perceived as good baffled me. Again, it's YouTube comments. Don't take them too seriously!

Having said all that, we felt we had a point to prove so we decided to take things up a notch in Division 3 and challenge Sunday league sides to send in a video explaining why they wanted to play us and why they felt they would beat us. If they thought they could smash us, then they could put their money where their below-the-video comment was and come and give us a game.

And, mate, would we get some games out of this.

# 8

# RETURN TO WEMBLEY

I had an itch I couldn't scratch, and it had nothing to do with Wembley Stadium.

Early in 2016 a mole on my arm was bugging me and, as my family has a history of skin cancer, I thought I'd better get it checked out at the doctors. It was only a little thing, but they sent me to hospital to have it removed, where I had my arm anaesthetised and a surgeon cut it out. I made sure I was looking the other way while they did it.

While the nurse was patching me up, I played the cheeky chappie and asked her when I could start playing football again. I couldn't believe what I heard.

'You need to have six weeks of doing nothing,' she said.

Six weeks for a measly little mole removed? Surely not. I had the Sidemen match coming up soon, not to mention my matches for Hashtag United.

'Can't I at least use the bike at the gym to keep fit and just rest my arm?' I said.

'Will you do me a favour?' the nurse said. 'Take a look at your arm.'

I did – and I nearly fell off my chair as I saw a hole the size of a tennis ball. 'What on earth is that doing there?' I whimpered.

Someone had messed up big style. The mole, it transpired, was benign – and I suspect somehow they thought it was cancerous when they cut it out, so they took a load of my flesh with it. My dad's had loads of moles removed and he's never had a scar like that. Working out what had gone wrong didn't really matter now, though. I was stuck with a great big hole in my arm.

It turned out the nurse was right about exercising. With an open wound like that, you're not supposed to get your heart rate up because it won't heal and you increase the chance of infection. And what did I do the day after the operation? Get straight on the exercise bike. After all, what did a trained medical professional know?

What should have taken a matter of weeks to heal became a matter of months. I soon accepted I'd have to stay out of the gym, but I couldn't avoid playing in Hashtag games, which is why if you watch some of those early videos I'm carrying a lot more weight than I am in later episodes.

By the time the Sidemen game came around at the start of June, my wound still hadn't healed. But I wasn't about to miss that match for anything.

The Sidemen were using Southampton Football Club's stadium, St Mary's, to put on a YouTubers match. Sidemen FC were taking on the YouTuber Allstars, and the best thing about it was that they'd sold 15,000 tickets for the match, so we'd be playing in front of a crowd.

The teams weren't that dissimilar to those that played the Wembley Cup, with KSI turning up for the Sidemen this time, and many of my teammates from that match, like ChrisMD and Joe Weller, playing for the Allstars. However, the Sidemen asked me to play on their team on this occasion.

Now, I like to think that's because they needed the inspirational leadership qualities of a Wembley Cup-winning captain on their side, but I think it's more likely that they were short of a centre-back so they thought I'd do. I even got a little bit of stick for playing for them – I was called 'snake' and 'traitor' in the comments. I could relate to what we'd put Manny through in the Wembley Cup but, at the end of the day, I didn't pick the teams. I was just really happy to be invited.

One thing I did bring to the team was some experience of playing in front of a crowd. With a crowd there, every time you do a good sliding tackle or shot, especially if you're near the sidelines or goal line, you look up and see people screaming your name, which is pretty cool. Of course, every time you muck up you'll see people going, 'Argh! What on earth are you doing?'

It's instant gratification, positive and negative, which is a massive departure from Sunday league where no one's really watching and only a few people care. It's like the difference between YouTube and TV, where you get the instant reaction in the comments below the video. If it's good, it's a hundred times better than when no one's watching, and if it's bad, well ...

After playing in the Legends match against Germany at Upton Park, I knew how loud you have to shout just to make yourself heard in front of a crowd. I spelled that out to the boys in the pre-match huddle – I *think* they could hear me over the crowd – and told them to yell themselves hoarse, because the crowd would be going crazy once the match started.

Whether my advice helped or not, you'd have to ask them, but I know I'd pretty much lost my voice by the end of the match from being so vocal throughout. That might have come as a bit of a relief to the boys!

What was a bit of a relief for me was to turn up to an event like this and not have to worry about any details of the production, like I have to at the Wembley Cup and for Hashtag games. For those games I rarely get to warm up properly because I have to do interviews with people, and I literally get a two-minute warm-up while all the other boys have a proper half-hour. It comes with the territory, as we're doing more than just playing a match, and I'm not complaining, but it was nice for a change to just turn up and play football. I loved it – except for one detail.

I played with that damn hole in my arm, and halfway through the match my bandage fell off . . . and then the special dressing underneath the bandage came off too. I was running around the pitch with the wind whistling through the hole in my arm, a really odd sensation. I got a second patch on in the second half and, because I was sweating so much, that came off too. It was pretty distracting, and I dreaded to think what the nurse from the hospital would have said.

The match itself was a great occasion. I think the Sidemen managed to get a few more hours' sleep than they did before the Wembley Cup, so people like MiniMinter were more able to show just how good they are at football. Our team won 7–2, and once again a few grumbles popped up about my always being on the winning team, but it wasn't like you could accuse me of running this particular show.

The game raised £100,000 for charity, which was a result in itself, and millions of people watched it on YouTube. There was some great football too, and the crowd were going mental. It was a fantastic day. Hats off to the Sidemen boys for putting it together. I went up to KSI at the afterparty and told him that I felt very proud to be a YouTuber that day.

I came out of that match with two thoughts in my mind. Firstly, I needed to let my arm heal and then get as fit as possible for what was going to be the biggest football match of my life: the second Wembley Cup.

And secondly, this year's Wembley Cup needed to be bigger and better than the last one – and it now had to top the Sidemen match, which had drawn an impressive crowd of 15,000 people.

Fitness first. Once the hole in my arm sealed and healed, I was determined to get into the shape of my life not only for the Wembley Cup, but for the upcoming milestone in my life, my 28th birthday. I told you I was old by YouTube standards.

So, exactly 100 days before my birthday, I started something called 100 Days of Fitness, in which I would do some form of exercise every day for those 100 days and post what I was doing on Instagram. My friend Jimmy Conrad, a YouTuber and former professional footballer, once told me that the coach never drops the fittest player in the squad. Sure, I might pick the Hashtag team, but it couldn't hurt to have that line of logic to back me up!

I know I can never get back the extra football experience other players my age have, but I know I can be fitter than them if I really put my mind to it. The way I like to see it is, given that I got into football late, it surely means that I would peak later and have a longer playing career (if that's not too grand a term for it!), well into my thirties. This is no doubt the same physical intuition that saw me riding an exercise bike the day after a surgeon gouged a hole out of my arm ...

I smashed it on the fitness front. One of the biggest reasons it worked was because I made myself accountable by putting it up on Instagram. If I missed a day, people would ask where my post was. I won't deny there were days I didn't fancy it, and probably didn't even need it, but I kept at it.

I've always eaten pretty well – I'm not bothered about sweet stuff and junk food – and I've never been the kind of guy to have a beer and watch the football. So I quit drinking alcohol altogether, and I've never looked back. It all added up, and I'd now say I'm definitely one of the fittest players in the Hashtag squad. Which is just as well, because I'm never going to be the best!

So with my fitness under control, I got together with EE and looked at how we could make this year's Wembley Cup a day that would top everything we'd done before.

We managed to get Wembley to agree to sell tickets for the match, which would give us a crowd of 20,000 on the day, and then we took a leaf out of the book of some of the teams I'd played against with Hashtag United and set about getting some ringers involved.

By teaming up with EA Sports, the makers of *FIFA*, we were able to recruit six legends for the teams, ex-pros who would hopefully lift the day to some dizzying new heights. As before, we would be building a series around the lead-up to our return to Wembley, but this time I wouldn't be up against MiniMinter and the Sidemen. I would be facing a team led by my former vice-captain Joe Weller. His Weller Wanderers would be taking on Spencer FC in the most spectacular Wembley Cup yet.

In the first episode we each recruited some familiar YouTube faces. My brother, Seb, was my first pick. He was desperate to play at Wembley again after getting a taste of it with Hashtag, and his new YouTube channel Seb on Golf now qualified him as a YouTuber!

I've mentioned that Seb loves his golf, but perhaps I haven't made clear how good he is at it. He's won the Trilby Tour – a national amateur golf tournament which is broadcast on Sky Sports – twice, the only person ever to do so. He's a seriously tough competitor who thrives on the big occasion, and I wanted him by my side at Wembley.

Joe Weller upped the ante by recruiting those seriously sick skillers the F2 Freestylers, as well as ChrisMD, Hurder of Buffalo and his good pal Theo Baker, while I got a freestyler of my own in the form of two-time Wembley Cup goal-scorer Daniel Cutting. I also got another very skilful player with Manny, but this time he'd be staying on my side for good!

Joe's team looked good but I did sense a lack of defenders in his squad, so I saw an opportunity. I got my old mates Poet and Vujanic, a defender and goalkeeper respectively, and the guys broke out into a rendition of our old Wembley Cup song in their own unique style.

Because Joe was available to appear in every episode of the series, we were able to do what we originally planned for the first Wembley Cup and build our teams together, onscreen, by doing challenges. The winner of the challenge would get the legend that was up for grabs in that episode, while the loser would get a YouTuber chosen by the public in a poll.

The first challenge was 'The Flying Squad', which would take place on the water. Vujanic was very quick to point out that, given that he wouldn't even jump in a puddle in the first series for fear of getting wet, it probably wasn't a wise move to have him on my team for this. That was a huge oversight on my part – I forgot that Vujanic was terrified of water and it was the production team's idea not to tell the lads what we were doing until we got down to the location.

Each person from the teams had to wear water-jet boots that would enable them to 'hover' in the middle of a lake in front of an inflatable goal and face three shots. The team who saved the most won the challenge. The prize? The legendary Manchester United goalkeeper Peter Schmeichel in the winner's team.

George Benson, who looked pretty comfortable out there, managed to save one for their team, and we were up next. Vujanic – an actual goalkeeper – stayed true to form with his aversion to water and chickened out once again, leaving me to make a complete mug of myself as I just couldn't get the hang of the hover boots. Unbelievably, I managed to keep one out, though it did come straight at me.

I needn't have worried about anyone remembering that, however, as Vujanic was eventually coerced into competing. He said no to the hover boots and instead crouched on a paddle board and tried to keep the shots out with his paddle. Poet was no better, bottling it and getting a ringer in his place – the former England goalkeeper David James, who was coaching us that day. Even his skills were of little use on the water, as Joe Weller and ChrisMD got the points to make sure Schmeichel was a Weller Wanderers player. First round to Joe.

Former Liverpool striker Robbie Fowler was the next legend up for grabs in the 'Gunk Tank' challenge, in which a player from one team aimed three shots at targets while his opponent stood in the gunk tank. Hitting the target would gunk the opposing player. Seb and the F2's Jeremy traded blows – and gunk – from six yards, before Joe and I proved we were both as bad as each other from 12 yards as we both exited the gunk tank without a drop of the sludgy stuff on us.

It was left to F2's Billy and Daniel Cutting to show us how it was done from 18 yards, and a gunk-soaked Billy won 2–1 in the battle of the freestylers, which meant Fowler would be turning out for Weller Wanderers at Wembley. And to rub salt – or at least some gunk – into my wounds, Billy and Jeremy gunked me F2-style, with an outrageous bit of skill before hitting the bull's-eye. I was soaked as I opened the public vote for my team between Caspar Lee and Joe Sugg. Another win for Joe but I wasn't too worried. His team might have been perfectly designed to win these YouTube challenges, but whether it would win him an 11-a-side game of football was another question indeed.

Robert Pirès was the prize for the third challenge, in which I'd take a team onto the 'World's Worst Football Pitch' against Joe's side. We had some expert coaching from Ray Parlour about how to deal with the surface. He'd thankfully calmed down after the drubbing Hashtag had dished out to the Vauxhall team he'd played in on a significantly better surface at Wembley. He'd probably forgotten all about it, and I wasn't going to bring it up ...

It really was the world's worst pitch: uneven, filthy, waterlogged in parts, more like a building site than a place for football, and probably not the best to be playing on to try to remain injury-free for a big upcoming match at Wembley! Thankfully, everyone remained unscathed, even if Jeremy managed to get himself booked, and the surface, while not quite nullifying the F2 boys' skills, at least made it a slightly more level playing field. Not literally, of course.

We managed to handle the conditions better and won the game 2–1. My first challenge victory, and what a prize –

Mr Robert Pirès. 'Magnifique, Spencer FC,' said the Arsenal and France legend.

'Action Replay' was a challenge in which each team had to re-create a legendary Wembley goal, namely Didier Drogba's incredible strike for Chelsea against Tottenham in the 2012 FA Cup semi-final. Plenty of kids up and down the country would have recreated that goal in their back gardens after the game, and we just had that little bit of extra pressure of the camera and our judge, former England striker Emile Heskey, holding up his score *Strictly Come Dancing*-style. The prize: the legend that is five-star skiller Jay-Jay Okocha.

It was close, but Joe Weller and the F2 Freestylers beat me, Daniel Cutting and Manny. We were disappointed but weren't too down about it: we knew there'd be no prizes for artistic merit at Wembley, where it would be all about the scoreline.

Seb and I took on Joe Weller and Theo Baker in the next challenge, called 'Strike Force', where we dribbled around a course and had to shoot at targets on the way. It was a close contest, and Seb did himself no favours at all by stacking it on his first shot and hurting his back, but it would take more than that to keep him out of Wembley. We won the challenge, and we got a legend we really needed for our team: former Netherlands international striker Patrick Kluivert. The team was coming together nicely, and it looked like it was going to be an incredible line-up at Wembley.

We did a poll asking the viewers which team people thought would win, and Joe was getting the backing on that – a big part of which, I assume, was because he had the F2 boys at his disposal. As the series went on, little seemed to change in the viewers' minds, judging by the below-the-vid comments. I was happy with the underdog status, and, just as I had with Hashtag United, I felt I was building a good all-round team.

Before the final pre-match episode, all that changed. Both the F2 boys were carrying injuries around this time. Billy was scheduled to have a hernia operation after the Wembley Cup, and Jeremy had a floating bit of bone around his ankle that needed an operation too. As they're a double act, it made sense for them to have their operations at the same time to minimise the amount of time they'd be out of action together.

The week before that episode, Jeremy's ankle went and he needed to have his operation straight away, which ruled him out of the Wembley Cup. The boys were then left to make a decision about whether Billy still played in the Wembley Cup, meaning the F2 would be out of action for longer, or bringing his operation forward to minimise the amount of time they'd miss as a double act. They chose the latter, which meant they were both out of the Wembley Cup.

We completely understood their decision, but we were gutted they wouldn't be there, as they're a great part of an occasion like that. They were gutted too – they love the Wembley Cup – and, given how good they are, it meant the teams had gone from Weller Wanderers looking like the better team on paper, to our side looking stronger.

Something needed to be done, but first there was the not-insignificant matter of the last legend to play for, and this was a particularly special one for a defensive player like me: Jamie Carragher, the absolute rock at the heart of Liverpool's defence for so many years and now popular pundit on Sky's football coverage.

I really wanted this one, not least because I knew getting Carragher in to play centre-back alongside Poet would free me up to play in a different position at Wembley, and when I learned that the challenge would be a *FIFA* match, I thought I had this one in the bag. Joe had never beaten me at *FIFA*. But then True Geordie, our presenter throughout the series, had a surprise for us. In shades of some of my early videos on my channel, it was to be a battle of the mums: Joe's vs my mum in a winner-takes-Carragher penalty shootout. The tension was unbearable …

Or at least it would have been if either of them could have figured out how to hit a penalty anywhere other than straight down the middle. It wasn't exactly YouTube gold, but

Joe's mum, who was an utter legend by the way, eventually succumbed to the might that is Sindy CB, and Carragher would be starting at Wembley for Spencer FC.

All of which stacked the odds against Weller Wanderers still further for the final, but he had some surprise reserve players ready for his team to make things fairer. My mate Jimmy Conrad, former captain of the USA national team, would tighten things up at the heart of the Weller Wanderers defence and effectively provide a fourth ex-pro for him, and YouTuber Elliot Crawford, who is a decent centre-back, would join his team too.

Now, you can't replace the F2 Freestylers in any YouTube team, sure, but in a way these changes were of benefit to Joe's team. He didn't have much of a defence before, and with us having players like Robert Pirès and Patrick Kluivert up against them we could have run riot. At least with Jimmy now marshalling his defence they'd have a more solid base.

But it was all just speculation by this point anyway. It was time to play the match.

● ● ●

I was determined to do everything I could to give our team the edge. Joe is a good mate and a great player, a lead-by-example type of captain, whereas I'm definitely not one of the best players in the team, so I have to make up for that in other ways – like trying to get the psychological edge.

On the day of the match our team were having lunch at one table in the hotel, while Joe and his team were sitting at another table. I decided to get up in the middle of eating and give a little speech to the team, firstly to bring everyone on my side together and feel included, because not everyone knew each other that well, and secondly because I knew Joe's team would be watching and thinking, *Hang on, why hasn't Joe done that for us?*

I even commented on the fact that they were watching us, and they'd be watching us on the pitch later winning the trophy, all as a bit of fun, really, but also all's fair in love and war and we were there to win. This kind of thing went on all day, but it was in the dressing room before the match that I delivered my most important words.

We had Patrick Kluivert, Jamie Carragher and Robert Pirès there for our pre-match talk. These guys have won all there is to win in football between them. I knew from experience that these games didn't mean an awful lot to players who had seen and done it all at the highest level. Playing at Wembley in front of 20,000 people just wasn't a big deal to them.

I wanted to make it clear that this wasn't just a corporate day out. This was the biggest game of our lives, and I wanted them to be motivated to play as well as they could because if they did, they'd be our heroes for ever.

So I said to them, 'It's an absolute privilege to be playing alongside World Cup winners, Champions League winners. It means a lot to us. Just to give you a little bit of context. This is our Champions League final. This is our World Cup final. It doesn't get bigger than this for us boys. So anything you can do to help us, use your skill, use your technique to help us get to the next level, we'll be eternally grateful. Let's get out there and let's win this!'

We all cheered. Maybe I was just imagining it from one defensive player to another, but I really felt like I might have got through to Jamie Carragher. Then again, it might just have been the pre-match adrenaline playing a few games with my own mind.

• • •

Walking out to a crowd of 20,000 people who would usually be separated from us by a computer screen or a phone was just incredible. Millions more were watching on YouTube too – more, in fact, than watched the Champions League final live on YouTube in the UK. This felt like a moment.

The match kicked off, and Seb and Manny combined well early on, with Manny flashing his shot just wide. Perhaps the indomitable presence of Manchester United legend Peter Schmeichel in bright-pink kit in the goal was enough to put him off.

Jamie Carragher made himself known to Joe Weller with the kind of strong challenge that had secured him legendary status at Anfield, but Joe wasn't the type to be subdued by that, and he started mouthing off at Carragher. All good-natured banter, of course. In fact, Joe had even indicated to me before the game that his game plan was to try to get in Carragher's head, something I felt might be a bad choice of strategy considering Carragher's mental fortitude.

From the resulting free-kick, some 30-plus yards out, Robbie Fowler fired it straight into the top corner. Vujanic couldn't blame his fear of water on this one – it was a great strike.

We came back strongly with our legends Patrick Kluivert and Robert Pirès linking beautifully, before Pirès finished it sumptuously. 1–1. Game on.

Daniel Cutting was busy trying to chip Peter Schmeichel every time he was through on goal, but the Great Dane wasn't to be beaten. And then Kieran Brown, then known as FootballSkills98, finished well for Wanderers after some good work from Theo Baker ... even if Vujanic may look back and feel he should have done better.

True Geordie put it cruelly in his commentary: 'One keeper is world class, the other is a YouTuber.' Ouch. No one has it tougher on the field than a keeper.

Speaking of world class, Jay-Jay Okocha was every inch the showman I'd both hoped and feared he would be, and he was running the show in midfield with some outrageous flashes of brilliance. He hit an absolute peach of a lob … which just sailed over. Close!

But anything a former professional footballer can do, a YouTube star can do better. Or at least they could in this match. Theo Baker picked up the ball in his own half and provided the greatest piece of magic of the match when he slalomed through our entire team, Poet, Jamie Carragher and all – I tried my best to get there from right-back but just couldn't quite make it in time to stop him – and finished smartly in what was surely one of the great Wembley goals (scored by a YouTuber). In fact, the goal was actually voted the best Wembley Stadium moment of 2016 in a public vote, beating playoff-final goals and Beyoncé concert performances in the process.

My initial reaction, after busting a gut to try to tackle him, was fury. How did we allow that to happen? But once I'd caught my breath, I had to take my hat off to him. Even though it was against my team, I look back on that moment fondly, watching a 20-year-old kid live out his wildest fantasy in front of a crowd at Wembley. Amazing. True Geordie's enigmatic commentary made it even better too – 'You've done it, son.' It gives me goose bumps whenever I watch it back, so I can't imagine how Theo feels.

Back to the game though, and we were 3–1 down. Not so amazing.

But we weren't out of it. Daniel Cutting had more luck as provider when he teed up Patrick Kluivert, who stroked a silky finish into the net from outside the box. The Dutchman wasn't doing much running on the pitch, but he was still a Rolls-Royce of a player, and that finish positively purred. Come on, boys!

Kluivert stepped up to remind Daniel that there's more than one way to beat the Great Dane when he converted a corner with a backheel that should be listed in the dictionary next to the word 'insouciant'.

The half-time whistle went and we headed to the dressing room with the scores level, but I was not happy. We weren't playing anywhere near as well as we could, and, after some wise words from the knowledgeable football manager we had for the day, former Arsenal defender Martin Keown, I gave some positive talk to the lads. But our biggest boost at half-time came from a more surprising source.

One of the producers of the show came into the dressing room and asked the legends, 'Is anyone OK to play 90 minutes?' The legends were only obliged to play 45 as part of their contract. Carragher immediately said, 'I'll play ninety.'

I just thought, *Get in!*

Now, there are a few reasons that Carragher might have been up for playing the full game, but I like to think it was at least partly due to the little speech I'd given before kick-off, setting out how important this match was to us. I think he'd got where I was coming from with that.

Another reason, of course, was that Joe Weller was really getting on his nerves. They'd been having a few verbals on the pitch, so Carragher seemed to say, 'Nah, I'm not having that. I'm going to have him in my pocket for the rest of the match.'

Either way, I was delighted, and most of the legends played more than the 45 minutes they were required to, which I thought was great from them. It showed they weren't just clocking on and off. But only Carragher played the full 90.

Much has been made of Carragher's aggression in this game, and while I think there might have been one or two moments where he got a bit carried away, there was a ref for a reason. It's the official's job to crack down on that sort of thing and nothing on the day was deemed worthy of a card in their eyes. I also think that when you're a retired centre-back who isn't as fast as he used to be, you need to use every trick in the book to stay on top of your opponents. Carragher definitely fell into that role but there's obviously a line that shouldn't be crossed. I wouldn't say Jamie crossed that line – I'd say he came very close to it – but all it showed to me was that he wanted to win the game and, being on his team, I appreciated that.

However, not even Champions League winner Jamie Carragher could stop us going 4–3 down at the start of the second half when Theo Baker got his second goal of the game, a far less spectacular finish than his first. We needed to steady the ship, and quick.

Kluivert, who didn't stop smiling all day, came close to a joyous hat-trick when he hit the bar with an effortless strike. ChuBoi put a lot more force into his shot that he blazed over soon after, but we finally broke their resistance when ChuBoi found his range and guided an equaliser in.

And then we won a penalty.

While Theo's goal was likely to be the best moment of the game for the viewers, the best moment for me was undoubtedly metaphorically handing the ball to my brother Seb to take the penalty that could give us the lead in the match. Football had brought us together as brothers and made us the firm friends we are today. Here we were, at Wembley Stadium, playing in a cup final together, with Seb about to put his name on the scoresheet.

He buried it, of course. We'd talked about doing the golf celebration before the match – we hadn't rehearsed it – because of his love of the sport, and we ran off and did it in the corner, just as we'd done so many other celebrations at home in our back garden as children. Only this time, 20,000 people were going berserk. What a feeling.

Seb would brag after the game about how he had a 100 per cent shot accuracy for the match. He managed one shot on target in the match and scored it. Stats don't lie!

We never looked back after that, with Manny adding a goal, and I was chuffed for another guy on our team who definitely couldn't boast of a 100 per cent shot accuracy after the chances he'd had, but who kept plugging away and putting himself in the right positions. Daniel Cutting finally buried a chance in injury time, proof that you can't keep a good man down.

The feeling of elation during the match, when you're just waiting for the whistle to go, there's nothing like it. The anticipation is almost the best bit. When the whistle goes, of course, my head switches out of game mode and into thinking about the video and the production.

But then I stopped, just for a moment, and reminded myself of that promise I'd made at the first Wembley Cup, that I would allow myself to drink it all in and enjoy it this time. And I did just that as we collected the trophy and celebrated like mad with the fireworks and glitter cannons going off. We even did a mini lap of honour with the trophy. If the first Wembley Cup had been the thing to put my channel on the map, this one was the cherry on top. It was oh-so sweet.

One responsibility I couldn't forget about, even for a moment, was the debt we owed the people who had made the day possible. The crowd had been amazing, and the great thing about it was that they weren't there just to support one team. Sure, some wanted Joe's team to win, while others wanted Spencer FC to, but they were there mainly to see a good show, which I hoped we'd delivered with 11 goals in total. There was none of the agro, hatred or bitterness you get from some types of football, just a really positive atmosphere with everyone out for a party.

I delivered my final speech of the day then, with a voice certainly more hoarse than before and motives undoubtedly more heartfelt than some of the mind games I'd been up to earlier. I thanked the amazing fans in the stadium and those watching on YouTube, whose support has never been less than incredible, as well as all the people who worked on the show, all the players – everyone involved.

I had to do that because, as with Hashtag, I have responsibilities beyond being just a player on the pitch. But more than that – much, much more than that – I was genuinely grateful.

These people had given me the greatest day of my life.

# 9

# #GRUDGEMATCH

We had challenged the cream of Sunday league sides around the country to send in a video explaining why we should play them, and the virtual mail bags at Hashtag United HQ were soon filled to bursting. We received videos saying everything from 'We'll smash you easily' to 'Our striker's better than your striker, so nah, nah, nah, nah, nah', and others unprintable in a book like this.

We would pick the best of them. We'd pay for their travel, put coaches or whatever they needed on to get down to the Hashtag Arena in north London, and we'd give them a game.

Division 3, in which we had a target of 18 points from 10 matches to get promoted, was going to be tougher than anything we'd experienced together as a team before. There was no danger of the teams we were about to play underestimating us or not taking it seriously, because they were challenging us and they knew full well what was on the line. They'd seen us play and they'd know what to expect.

Added to that, these teams had been playing together for years, whereas we had only been together for a few months. Sure, some of us went way back, but this squad, as a collective, with the new boys Seb had brought into the fold that we were only just getting to know, hadn't been together long. It takes time to forge proper understandings, and experience to fully meld a group together. I knew we had some good players, but I wasn't sure that would be enough.

To be brutally honest, I thought we were going to get stuffed.

Our first match was against the Fox and Hounds FC, a team that had won the double in the Watford Sunday league the previous season, scoring 175 goals in the process and barely conceding. The thing about Sunday league is that you can't always gauge the level teams are playing at, but on paper they'd smashed it – and now they wanted to take a pop at us.

The Sunday league theme wasn't the only thing we changed to kick off Division 3. We had a deal with a new shirt sponsor, too, *Top Eleven*, a very popular mobile management game, and we were delighted. EE had been great to us, but it was only ever a short-term deal, and they'd had some exposure from it and we'd had a sponsor on our shirts. It was an amicable split.

The *Top Eleven* deal was a gamechanger for us. Up until this point, I had been paying for everything out of my own money.

The costs were fairly substantial. I'd have four cameramen on each shoot, the pitch-hire fee, equipment costs, paying the refs (yes, we do pay them!) and linesmen – it all adds up – which for amateur football is pretty crazy. I definitely wasn't making that back in advertising revenue on YouTube.

I think some people had the wrong idea about Hashtag and thought we were this YouTube team set up to make money, but in actual fact I was losing money every game. I definitely wasn't complaining, though. Hashtag was an investment, and any money we had coming in went straight back into making more content and paying for things like travel when we hit the road.

It was never guaranteed to be a success. The whole project was a gamble for me, but it was a risk worth taking because I got to do some cool things with my mates, and I was hopeful that, if it worked, a sponsorship deal would follow. *Top Eleven* gave us that deal and they have been brilliant. The cherry on the cake was that our badge and kits would be integrated into the *Top Eleven* game itself, as well as some of our videos. Slowly but surely, Hashtag United were taking over the virtual football-management world!

We made some tweaks to the format of the videos, to keep things fresh for the viewers. We added in the 'Previously on Hashtag United … ' recap section at the start, just like the 'here's what happened last time' bits on a quality drama series. We also added pre- and post-match interviews against an advertising-board background – just like you'd see in broadcast-TV football coverage – to make things look that little bit more slick, and hopefully get some decent words from those involved in the games. This was an effort to bring the personalities of some of our players into the content more and make it less about Spencer and more about Hashtag.

The Chairman was upping the ante too. He promised us a new signing if we got promoted, which set YouTuber tongues wagging as to who that might be, and on a more worrying note he promised that, if we were relegated from the division, we would lose a player, chosen by a public vote. Uh-oh …

Sam Leete, the Fox and Hounds manager, certainly had some confident words in his pre-match interview, predicting a 3–0 scoreline, but words can only take you so far in this game, and it was the talking we would do on the pitch that mattered.

The match against the Fox and Hounds was tough. They were a good side, really well organised, but we were up to the task. Ryan Adams scored with a very neat finish to give us the lead and, for the first time in a Hashtag shirt, we kept a clean sheet to give us a 1–0 win. The Chairman was delighted with the clean sheet in particular.

We were good value for the win too. Sam 'brother of Ryan' Adams was superb at the back for us, with Dan Brown and Ryan, our dream-team strikers, buzzing around and causing them problems all match, and John Dawson, playing in central midfield next to me, absolutely clobbering the bar with a shot. The Fox and Hounds had arrived bigging up their goal-scoring exploits, but their goalkeeper was probably their most impressive performer.

With the first three points in Division 3 now secure, we received an update direct from the Sky Sports News office. The breaking news was in, and the headline read: SKY SPORTS NEWS HQ CHALLENGE YOU TO A MATCH. SEE YOU ON THE FOOTBALL PITCH.

The Sky Sports News team had followed a pretty similar trajectory to Hashtag in many ways, playing games against Premier League clubs' staff teams and those of other media outlets. They were a proper team in their own right and they'd done their homework on Hashtag, watching every game we'd played, and they certainly weren't going to be treating it like an exhibition match.

Despite this being Sky Sports, they were a Sunday league side consisting of people who worked there. There were no famous faces in their ranks – just a team of good footballers – and that's much scarier to me than a team with some ex-pros in them. With all due respect to the Graeme Le Sauxs of this world, they might still have incredible technique, but we could just run round them. They're not in their physical prime any more, and they just don't care as much.

I was definitely proven right on that. The Sky Sports News team were very good indeed, and from the start we found ourselves under the cosh. They were absolutely all over us, and I don't think we'd been dominated to such an extent before.

It was an evening kick-off, and as the day slowly faded and the floodlights snapped into action, we knew we were in for a real game here. We had to keep things tight at the back. I found myself resorting to hoofing it long just to relieve a bit of the pressure, and with Dan and Ryan up front, chasing everything down, it wasn't the worst tactic in the world.

With some of the players we have in our team, you can never write us off. After some magic from John Dawson on the left, Dan Brown managed to gobble up a rebound and put us 1–0 up. The goal was completely against the run of play, and the pressure wasn't about to let up any time soon.

The rest of the match followed a similar pattern, with Sky Sports dominating possession and Hashtag looking to hit them on the break. Our goalkeeper, Andy Jeffs-Watts, played a blinder, and Sky Sports could rightly feel frustrated as we kept them at bay. However, we had our chances too, and we came desperately close to putting the game out of sight with a couple of slick counter-attacks.

It was dark by the time the whistle went and we'd secured our second 1–0 win in the division, with only our second-ever clean sheet. We could not believe we'd won, and as we trudged off the pitch tired but over the moon in a way only a hard-earned win can make you feel, there was a sense that things were beginning to click with this team.

We'd been together as a group for a little while now. There were a load of boys in the group who knew each other from school and our CBA days, of course, but we were really getting to know Seb's mates too, and we were getting on better than I'd ever dreamed we would. Nothing brings a team together more than winning, of course, but it wasn't just that.

We had a WhatsApp group going with loads of banter flying around every day, and looking forward to the next game was becoming a huge part of our lives, not just mine. The guys couldn't wait for the end of their working week when they could pull on the Hashtag shirt once again. We were in this together.

There was a feeling in the group that we had a bit of a Leicester City 2015–16 thing going on. Leicester, of course, had won the Premier League the previous season against all odds, and we could see some similarities in our squad. We were playing a relatively unfashionable 4–4–2 formation in which our two frontmen were getting all the goals, just like Leicester. We were a counter-attacking side too as well as having this incredible camaraderie going on, just like the Foxes in the Premier League. Most of all, we were beating teams we had no right to beat on an incredible roll that showed no signs of stopping.

So of course we lost our next game, against one of the weaker Sunday league teams we had played. All that Leicester

City rubbish we had been talking about the week before went out the window pretty quickly, didn't it?

Mongolian Horses FC were a Sunday league side captained by Matt Stevens, brother of our midfielder James Stevens. This match was as much about family pride for the Stevens boys as anything else, but there were still three points up for grabs so there were no excuses for taking it lightly. And, with all due respect to Matt and his team, given the teams we'd beat we never should have lost this match.

Having said that, we shouldn't have gone in front the way we did either. Their goalkeeper made an absolute howler in the ninth minute, coming to collect a regulation ball and somehow letting it through his legs to allow Ryan Adams to nip round and score the easiest goal anyone is likely to score in a Hashtag shirt. Seriously, who would be a keeper?

We came out for the second half and realised just what an opportunity we'd passed up in the first. It was really windy that day, with the sun low in the sky. We'd had the wind and the sun behind us in the first half, but now we were playing into the elements, and it was very hard to see and to get the ball out. I could sympathise with their keeper now, as we were really up against it.

With just 15 minutes to go, we completely fell apart. We conceded two goals in five minutes, with the second a real blow for the Stevens family bragging rights as Matt Stevens outmuscled his older brother to score it. And then they added a third – a great free-kick, to be fair – to finish the game as a contest.

We could point to things like the weather and to Dan Brown and Rich Beck, two stalwarts of the side, being missing for the match, but that's no excuse. They had to deal with the weather in the first half, just like us, and illness, injury and suspensions happen to players throughout a season. It's how you deal with them as a squad that counts.

I think we'd just got a bit cocky. When Leicester lost Jamie Vardy to suspension during the run-in of their title win, other players stepped up and they got results in their big games. We had a little way to go yet before those Leicester comparisons we'd been making were in any way valid.

We got back to winning ways against AC Belmont, thrashing them 8–1 in a match that featured the first sending off in any of our games. When we were 5–1 up, Seb rented a bit of space in a couple of their players' heads – he was making a bit of a pest of himself – and they just lost it. Their keeper took a swipe at him first, getting booked and giving away a penalty in the process, which Rich Beck coolly converted.

Another of their players threw the ball away and was booked for it, and then seconds later he had a swipe at Seb too and got his second yellow card for that. My brother is a merciless competitor and can be a real nuisance on the field, but you have to be able to deal with that, and these players clearly couldn't. They left the ref with little choice but to get the cards out.

Now, as I've mentioned, the referees and linesmen we use in Hashtag matches are all fully qualified, decent officials who are used to presiding over a much higher level of football than we're playing.

In our early matches, they thought it was all just a bit of fun and they didn't take it too seriously. They were a bit too relaxed for our liking, and I think they got a real shock when they saw us going mental when we scored – or for different reasons when decisions didn't go our way – and realised what it meant to us.

I had to say to them, 'Can you please treat these games like a cup final? You need to take this seriously because we really care about this, the people we're playing care about this and the fans at home do too. You might not be aware of it, but in terms of audience numbers, this is the biggest game you've ever refereed. Go to my YouTube channel and have a look at how many hundreds of thousands of people are watching and scrutinising every single one of your decisions.'

They tended to get it after that, and now the refs are all on board with it and do their best. They're usually decent, but just like goalkeeping, being a ref is a thankless task. Booking players is part of the job, no matter whose side they're on, and we wanted officials to be impartial and professional because these games were everything to us.

We weren't expecting anything to be easy about our game against NWA, a football club from north-west London that unsurprisingly didn't feature Ice Cube and Dr Dre up front. They were in fact a group of mates who had each played at a very high youth level and they had a bit of a social-media presence. They also had an eloquent, ambitious manager and a very impressive montage of goals on their challenge video that made me think, *These guys are unbelievable.*

Now, you should never base an opinion of a player on his YouTube highlights reel, but these guys were the real deal, certainly more than good enough to mug me off a few times on the pitch! We went 2–0 down in the first half and I thought, *Oh no, this is it. This is where we finally get smashed.*

A part of me thought we needed that and the series needed that ... but the rest of me, the competitive part of me embroiled in a really tough game, definitely did not want to lose this match. Like the match against Mongolian Horses, it was a really windy game with the sun sitting low in the sky. We were playing into the wind and facing the sun, and we couldn't see a thing. But that was no excuse.

If we could just hang in here, maybe nick something before half-time ...

Cometh the hour, or at least the minute before half-time, cometh the man, and Ryan Adams managed to squeeze a shot under their keeper and throw us a lifeline. At half-time I told the lads I was sure we could turn this around. We came out for the second half only 2–1 down – and with the sun strong in the eyes of the NWA defence and the wind blowing firmly in favour of Hashtag United. We'd learned our lesson from the Mongolian Horses game. We needed to use the elements to our advantage this time.

It didn't take long, as minutes into the second half John Dawson scored what was voted the best Hashtag goal of the year with an absolute belter from 30 yards. Sam Adams then gave us the lead after some head tennis in the box, and it was all Hashtag from then on, with no little help from the sun.

We had reason to be unhappy with the officials who ruled a Dan Brown effort out for offside, despite being about four yards onside, but there was no stopping us. Dan eventually got his goal with a sweet finish and we won the game 5–3, which was an incredible result against a very good team of genuinely decent players. We'd really turned up, and what a comeback!

Our next match was a tricky away fixture at Newhaven FC, the under-21s side of a semi-pro team, who had some very familiar faces in their ranks. Theo Baker and Joe Weller were lining up against us and they were out for revenge after they'd lost in the Wembley Cup, and to make things even more interesting, we were playing in front of a crowd for the first time as a club.

We were missing a couple of key players for the match, with Phil Martin and the Adams brothers unavailable, but we'd learned our lesson from last time. We recalled midfielder Jack Harrison for the occasion, and, with Sam Adams missing at the back, the Chairman sorted out a very special loan signing: Mr Jimmy Conrad, former USA captain and World Cup player. Playing at Newhaven might be a bit of a first for Jimmy, too.

Joe Weller wasn't at his best as he was suffering from an injury in this game, which would eventually keep him out for the best part of a year as he ended up needing surgery. However, despite Joe not being 100 per cent, Newhaven still had a really good side. It was a tough game played in freezing-cold conditions down by the coast, but in the end we had a little too much for them. We're a bit older than those boys so we were able to physically boss them a little bit, and our extra experience counted as we won the game 2–1. Dan Brown was in inspired form as he bagged a brace.

Another factor in the match, which we had definitely learned to deal with by now, was the cameras. While we no longer had the advantage of other teams not taking it quite as seriously as us, we did have the experience of playing regularly and being filmed with hundreds of thousands of people watching on

YouTube. Even in our team talks, the lads barely even noticed the cameras were there by this stage because we were so used to it. It had become second nature to us.

A lot of the teams we played weren't used to being filmed, so they were out of their comfort zone. Joe and Theo are young lads but old hands by YouTube standards and they'd played in the Wembley Cup, so the cameras were hardly a problem for them, but for their teammates it was a new experience, and some of them might have been a bit dazzled by the lights. According to Joe in his post-match interview, his teammates might have been worrying a bit too much about what people on YouTube were going to say rather than having their heads 100 per cent in the game.

I could relate to finding the cameras distracting. It was why I had Saunders in charge of the production because once the whistle goes, I only want to be thinking about the match. We were playing some very good teams, and if my head wasn't in the game I'd be mugged off very publicly. Sometimes I'm still mugged off anyway! You can't afford to have any distractions once the whistle goes if you want to give the best account of yourself.

We only needed three more points to secure promotion, and we had our chance against a team that broke with the Sunday league theme of the division, but would still offer us an extremely tough game.

Daniel Cutting, my teammate in the Wembley Cup, had put together a team of freestylers to challenge us. I was well up for this, because with freestylers, yes, they might have some unbelievable skills, but you're never quite sure just how good they are at playing the game itself. How would they gel as a unit? Is it possible to be both a freestyler and an uncompromising centre-back?

I knew Daniel was a very good player, but a whole team of freestylers?

It turned out they were very good. A lot better than we expected, in fact. We found ourselves 3–2 down with only 10 minutes to go, and I was watching from the sidelines with a dead leg as the big man James Stevens, who had replaced me on the field, set up the equaliser for Dan Brown. We wouldn't be getting promoted in this match after all, but it did feel like we'd got ourselves off the hook and salvaged a point against a team who were playing their first ever match together. Fair play to the Freestylers – they were decent.

We hit the road again for another away match, this time against Biggleswade United, on a grass pitch so that any advantage we might have gleaned from playing on our 3G artificial surface, which we'd had plenty of practice on by now, wasn't a factor. This was a big one, too. It was our sponsor *Top Eleven*'s derby: the two teams they sponsored would be playing.

Biggleswade are a semi-pro team with a very special director of football in Guillem Balagué, the Sky Sports presenter. He sent in the challenge and promised a very interesting match-up, with him playing up front.

When we played semi-pro teams, this was usually the case. As good a unit as I felt we were becoming – we had a few guys in our ranks who had played semi-pro and one or two who could no doubt play it – we were still amateur footballers. We wouldn't stand much of a chance against a semi-pro first XI, and while some people might love to see us get smashed in the videos, it wouldn't make for much in the way of entertainment every episode.

So a semi-pro team would usually put an XI together with a few first-teamers, a few under-21 players, maybe some staff and a star or celebrity performer, like Guillem, for the match. In the case of a club like Biggleswade, that's still a very decent team, and they had another very familiar face in their starting line-up: former Barcelona and Chelsea midfielder Enrique de Lucas. Make no mistake, this was going to be a tough game.

We were proudly sporting rainbow laces for the match as part of an anti-homophobia in sport campaign, and I was also sporting my Movember moustache as part of the men's health charity campaign for the month.

It was an overcast day down at Biggleswade, with the floodlights on to illuminate events on the pitch. The scores were level at 1–1 with half-time approaching, when de Lucas received a good pass, got past Rich Beck . . . and then the man-mountain brought him down in the box. Penalty!

Who else but Guillem Balagué stepped up to take it, and he struck it firmly enough, but Jamie 'Jacko' Jackson in goal pulled off an amazing stop, pushing it away for us to launch a counter-attack. I hit it long and left Dan Brown and Ryan Adams to take care of the rest, as they combined superbly, with Ryan breaking away and having his shot parried by the keeper, and Dan there to follow up. Unbelievable!

From staring down the barrel of a 2–1 deficit at the break, we were now 2–1 ahead – all in a matter of seconds. It was a real #MiseryCompiler for Biggleswade.

Things just got better and better after the break. I rolled back the years to my school days, when my heading prowess was enough to get me noticed, and I scored a pretty decent header. Best of all, it was the Manjdog himself who supplied the brilliant cross: great link-up play between the two founders of the Hashtag United seven-a-side team to put us 3–1 up.

We then ran over to the side to do a haircut celebration. I'd done a big Movember charity stream in which we raised the best part of $60,000 for the charity, and as part of the incentives to donate I'd said that I wouldn't get my hair cut until I scored for Hashtag. Given that I hadn't scored since we demolished the comedians' team by a margin of 18 goals, the odds were pretty strong on my locks getting very long indeed.

I'd been getting a fair bit of stick for rarely scoring, so it was a good challenge for me, but, unbelievably, I'd scored in only my second match since making the claim. However, it would be a little while longer before I made a trip to the barbers!

My goal wasn't the only thing I had to celebrate by the end of the match. Despite Biggleswade drawing things level at 3–3, we went ahead and finished the game strongly. We won 6–3, and secured promotion to Division 2, as well as the new star signing promised by the Chairman, in the process.

We finished 2016 off with the Hashtag United Awards, a great evening with the lads at YouTube HQ and an opportunity to swap the yellow-and-blue kit for black tie. We handed out the player awards for the year, including the players' player of the year, which went to top goal-scorer Dan Brown, while the fans' player of the year went to his strike partner, second-top scorer and leading assist-maker for the year Ryan Adams. I told you they were the dream team. John Dawson won goal of the year for *that* strike against NWA.

Being solid at the back had been just as vital to our success, however, and the Chairman, who loved a clean sheet, certainly recognised this when he made the man-mountain himself, Mr Rich Beck, the Chairman's player of the year. The Chairman, of course, couldn't be there in person, but he talked it through with me before the ceremony.

At the climax of the awards we revealed the Chairman's new star signing. And it was a familiar face to the YouTube community: Theo Baker. He would be wearing the number 77 shirt, and he showed signs of fitting right in as he Hashtagged it on stage in front of the lads. Theo's a great player and it was a brilliant signing for us and, as ever, collaboration was the name of the game. We would both enjoy some exposure on one another's channels. It was a fantastic night, and we looked forward to life in Division 2 with confidence.

Of course, given the realities of how we make the show, filming the matches in advance of showing them, we'd already kicked off Division 2 at this point. And we'd done it with a bang, delivering the YouTube match-up everyone had been waiting for: Hashtag United vs Palmers FC. You wouldn't want to miss this one . . .

• • •

Every drama needs a good villain. Every hero needs their nemesis. Superman has kryptonite. Batman has the Joker. The FIFA Playa has KSI. And for Hashtag United, we had Palmers FC. The stakes were high, with YouTube supremacy at stake, and for the first time in a Hashtag shirt, things were about to get properly nasty.

We'd been getting comments about how a team called Palmers FC would smash us if we played them, with people saying stuff about how they played in a 'real' league, which sort of missed the point of what we were trying to do with Hashtag.

As for these 'real' leagues, I know all about them. I've turned out in teams in them for years and I know the kind of football that's played, so there was nothing there really to fear, despite what some people might claim.

We got in touch with Palmers to challenge them to a game quite early on and, to be fair, if we'd played them then, without building the understanding and camaraderie in our team that only comes from experience, who knows what the result would have been. But we were doing something different to clubs like Palmers: we'd already played at Wembley, and I was looking to do something cool on YouTube with my mates. I didn't want to get into Sunday league. I felt like that had been done.

Division 3, with its Sunday league theme, was our answer to that, and we'd proven we could mix it with these teams. By the time our match with Palmers came round, the comments were no longer an unequivocal 'Palmers will smash you'. In fact, there was a genuine bit of interest in the game because we'd changed quite a few opinions with our performances. The thought of a good match between two decent YouTube teams was an exciting one for followers of both Hashtag and

Palmers, and we could hardly disappoint our subscribers now, could we?

From day one, it was clear that Palmers didn't like us, whether it was sending incendiary tweets or making little digs about us in their own videos. All good friendly banter, of course, and we'd respond in kind sometimes and it seemed like fun. Two YouTube teams creating a bit of theatre around the game, almost like the pre-fight promotion of a boxing match. Bring it on.

Sometimes it went a little too far – from both sides. We originally organised to play them much earlier, but we had to cancel that match because the second Wembley Cup ended up being scheduled two days later. I couldn't play any game two days before the Wembley Cup. If I'd got injured, I would have let a lot of people down involved in the production of the Wembley Cup series.

So we told the Palmers guys we'd have to reschedule, hoping they'd understand and we could arrange a new date. And they seemed to at first, but then they'd go on Twitter and try to throw me under the bus, suggesting we were running scared because we cancelled. We challenged them in the first place!

I'd come back with a bit of banter, something like, 'We're cancelling because we're playing at Wembley – where are you playing, Thurrock Sunday league pitch?' All good-natured fun, but I could definitely sense a bit of venom coming our way.

You're probably sick of hearing me use the 'c' word by now – 'collaboration', that is – but that really is the key to making these things work on YouTube. That's why the Wembley Cup works so well, with all these big YouTubers collaborating. And it should have been like that with Palmers and us, two sides with a YouTube presence, but I think a bit of football tribalism was creeping into it.

We have our genuine supporters and Palmers have theirs, and they each felt passionately about wanting to see their team win. I think that, combined with the needle between the two sides in the build-up, as well as the knowledge that Palmers were a very physical side, meant we had the perfect storm brewing for a real winner-takes-all grudge match.

To make the match an extra-special occasion, we sold tickets for it – the first crowd at the Hashtag arena – and we had around 500 people there watching, with all the proceeds going to the charity Movember. Theo Baker would also be making his debut and, let's not forget – and it was easy to do it in the atmosphere that was building – three points were up for grabs in a division in which we'd need 20 points in 10 games for promotion.

Palmers are your archetypal kick-you-off-the-park Sunday league team. Don't get me wrong, they've got some decent players, but we knew they would be physical and we knew they really didn't like us. I think they felt we'd come into their territory somehow when in reality we were operating in an entirely different space. Maybe they were jealous? I'm not sure, but the atmosphere was far from friendly that day. We didn't hate them – they were just another opponent to us. Like any half-decent team, we've got the sort of players who can mix it when things get physical, and we knew we'd have to match them in that regard, as well as play some good football, otherwise they'd walk all over us.

All of which meant it was a difficult game for the referee. We came in at half-time 1–0 down and a little surprised that our midfielder John Dawson had been the first player to be booked, given the challenges that had been flying around. We might have been raising money for charity but there was precious little sense of that on the pitch. They had really celebrated their goal, a close-range header that gave Andy in goal little chance. It clearly meant something to them.

There was no Martin Keown around to tell me to keep it calm this time as I gave my half-time team talk. I was desperate for us to just try to keep it a bit more simple, to play the straightforward first pass, and tried my best to get that message across.

One shrewd thing we did do was to bring on midfielder Jack Harrison. Now, Jack's a really good player, but not everyone who has watched our games will necessary have picked up on that. He was captain of England Independent Schoolboys in his youth and he'd been in the squad a lot, but he wasn't always available for games. Remember, these boys are amateur footballers, which means they have jobs to go to and other commitments. I hadn't picked him for the starting XI because we'd been winning, and you don't break up a winning team, but this was his chance to show us what he could do.

He didn't disappoint. He came on and really made a difference, and we were by far the better team in the second half, with Palmers sitting back, trying to protect their lead. There was still plenty of physical stuff going on – and plenty of handbags, too – but we weren't going to allow that to distract us. Dan Brown finished beautifully in a crowded penalty area to bring the scores level, and we celebrated wildly. It clearly meant something to us too.

With just over 10 minutes to go, Jack Harrison capped off a gamechanging display with a goal. It wasn't the cleanest contact on the ball, but it didn't need to be, perhaps fittingly for a game like this, and it was the least we deserved for our performance.

We still had to see the remainder of the game out, and things got quite bad-tempered and silly before the end. Rich Beck, the man-mountain, was rightly booked for his efforts to stop a free-kick being taken quickly, putting one of the Palmers players down in the process, and then a bit of nonsense kicked off before the whistle was finally blown.

What a relief. We'd won the battle of the YouTuber teams and earned the bragging rights, but it had been tough – hard-fought, bad-tempered at times and undoubtedly the most physical game Hashtag had played by far.

The officials hadn't had the best of games, as Palmers felt aggrieved by a couple of offside decisions, and I was not happy that we'd received two bookings and none had gone their way, especially given the challenges they'd been putting in. Ryan Adams had been elbowed twice and there were two instances on me that should have been straight reds, in my opinion.

But the whistle had gone and the game was over. The 500 people in attendance had witnessed a firm but fair match – shout-out to them by the way for not only raising so much money for charity, but also braving the blistering cold that night. It was a tight game that could have gone either way. Smiv, who doesn't play but films and edits the Palmers content, had a good view of the proceedings and he was gracious enough at the time to say that we deserved the victory.

Beating Palmers saw us rise to the top of the YouTube tree as the number-one side on the platform – a place I felt we already were, to be fair, but this had proved it. There were always going to be people who wouldn't be converted, and those who preferred to watch the Sunday league experience on

YouTube, and that's cool with us. We're not trying to pinch that audience – it's never been us or them. I'd say, 'Watch us and watch Palmers, or Manny's Eltham or ChrisMD's Sunday League Experience – we do different things and it's all great.'

If you want to see a really good representation of what happens in Sunday league, watch some of these channels. If you want to watch a bunch of mates living their crazy dream and playing in stadiums they're nowhere near good enough to set foot in, and going up against players we have no right to, then watch us. Watch us all, if you like!

The most important thing to us was that we'd won and silenced some critics in the process. Now we could move on from silly comments questioning our ability. I've gone on record time and time again saying that we're nothing special football-wise. All beating Palmers did was prove that we were better than them, and that we were certainly good enough to play in Sunday league if we wanted to. That was enough for me.

Next up: we had plans to take Hashtag United to dizzying new heights. Quite literally, as we planned flights to Northern Ireland and the USA. Hashtag United were about to go international.

# 10

# GOING INTERNATIONAL

Today, eSports is big business. All around the world millions of people are tuning in online to watch some of the best players take each other on at games such as *League of Legends* and *DotA 2* for serious prize money. It's treated as a national sport in some places, particularly in countries like South Korea, with stadiums full of people watching the players battle it out in the flesh.

This might sound mad to some of you, but it shouldn't for too much longer; eSports is basically just competitive gaming, and it is one of the fastest-growing sports in the world. Whether you consider it an actual sport or not could well determine which side you're on of the generational divide that had my dad telling me I could have been great at snooker!

The football-game side of eSports has been pretty slow in coming to the party. I started commentating on some

*FIFA* eSports tournaments back in 2014, and no one was coming to watch. There were people watching online, of course, but nothing like the numbers that other video games were drawing. I would work at events where there were only a handful of fans watching on our *FIFA* stage, but down the hall there would be thousands of people going mental and cheering on their favourite players at *Call of Duty*. I wondered why.

I love commentating at these events. I could easily have said no to it as I had my hands full at the time, but I was really interested in doing it. I was already doing commentary over my own *FIFA* games and I was up for the challenge of doing it as a neutral for an audience in a competitive sport.

It opened up a new world to me. I got to know a lot of the players and see all the nuances of *FIFA* eSports. Knowing how popular a game *FIFA* was, with such a huge amount of people playing and watching videos by the likes of me, KSI and plenty of other YouTubers besides, I thought there was huge potential in this.

I really wanted to be part of it and I had to get in early with it. There were no real *FIFA* eSports teams around, and I had a hunch that EA Sports – the makers of the game – were going to invest more in this area. It made sense for them to try to turn *FIFA* into one of the world's biggest eSports, and I saw an opportunity.

When I created Hashtag United, it was not only with the aim of making a real football club with my mates, but also with the intention to build a *FIFA* eSports team.

The appeal was simple. It was going to take years to build a real football club from scratch and take it to the heights I really dreamed for it, but with an eSports team I could, with just a few smart moves, potentially have the number-one team in the world much quicker.

I wanted to do it creatively, however. I wanted to get some great content out of it and use the reach I had on my channel to generate some interest in it. By this point, early in 2016, I was working hard to up the production values on my shows considerably.

I had started a new series called *Bench Warmers*, which was basically my version of a TV panel show, a bit like *A League of Their Own* but for a YouTube audience, with YouTubers on the panel. We got 'The Beast', Adebayo Akinfenwa, on one episode, and in later shows we'd get special guests like Tottenham and England midfielder Dele Alli and West Ham's Reece Oxford. The show was made in a studio in London in front of an audience and looked – or at least I hope it did – like it wouldn't be out of place on TV.

I looked to TV again for inspiration when it came to building my eSports team. *Game Academy* was my version of

*The Apprentice*, in which I would play the Alan Sugar role, taking a group of ten young hopefuls keen to be the first signing for my eSports team through a series of challenges and eliminations over several episodes before the final two duked it out for a 12-month contract on my team.

To find our contestants, we teamed up with an online gaming website called Gfinity. Everyone joining this website had to play in a qualification bracket and, of the 12,000 people competing, we picked the top ten for the show. *Game Academy* was how I first got involved with Umbro, too, who helped fund the show. It would prove to be a useful contact for the Hashtag United kit.

The standard of the applicants was seriously high, and I was handed some real beatings as I played the contestants. After six episodes and an awful lot of *FIFA*, we got down to the final two, Harry Hesketh and Kieran Brown. First they had to endure the classic interview episode – with Alex and Seb doing the grilling on my behalf, much like Karren Brady and Claude Littner do for Lord Sugar on *The Apprentice* – and then they played in the Gfinity *Play Like a Legend* Grand Final event before the guys went head to head.

And what a final it was. Harry Hesketh came from behind to snatch victory in a pulsating encounter in added time. He won the 12-month contract to be our first eSports player, and as I handed him his official Hashtag United shirt I could see big things in this kid's future. Hashtag Harry had a very nice ring to it.

We added three more players, with Tassal Rushan, Ivan Lapanje and Dirty Mike, or Hashtag Mike as he's now known, joining Hashtag Harry in the eSports team. You might remember Mike's mum playing my mum at *FIFA* on my channel, and Mike would represent Hashtag United at the American tournaments. With two UK players, a Swede and an American, we really had gone international!

We'd put together what I considered to be the best *FIFA* eSports roster in the world, and people like Harry have exceeded all expectations. At the *FIFA 17* Ultimate Team European regional final in Paris, Tass won the whole tournament, beating the cream of professional *FIFA* players in the process and qualifying for the Ultimate Team Championship final in Berlin in May 2017. He also earned a cheeky $30,000! Harry, Ivan and Mike all qualified for regionals too, which is an amazing achievement when you consider how competitive the qualification process on FUT Champions is.

The sport itself was growing. The total prize money in the European final was $100,000, and at the Ultimate Team Championship final it was $400,000, more than ten times what the big events had been paying out in previous years. Not only that, but BT Sport and ESPN were broadcasting the finals so they'd be on TV, not just online. The 'real' world was starting to take note.

This surge of interest of course attracted other people who wanted a slice of the action, and that's great for the sport. Clubs like Paris Saint-Germain (PSG) and Wolfsburg in Germany have invested heavily in eSports teams, while West Ham were the first Premier League club to do it, and I was happy to help them get it off the ground. I was even happier to see Manchester City sign Kieran Brown, who was the runner-up in *Game Academy*. A few of the other applicants from the series have gone on to be signed by pro teams and perform well at events too. Pretty good for a load of unknowns! Maybe we should do another one ...

The *FIFA* tournaments take place all around the world – it's a truly international affair – and you have players fighting it out on the consoles wearing their club colours. So there will be players in PSG, Wolfsburg, Man City, Ajax or Schalke shirts ... and some wearing a Hashtag United kit. It's incredible!

These players are all paid a salary – so they don't have to get jobs and can spend all day getting better at *FIFA* – and then they win prize money on top. It's not the kind of money that pro *League of Legends* or *DotA* players get right now, but it's a dream job for some people. Obviously, we can't afford to compete financially with the PSGs and Man Citys of this world with our wages, but we can offer our players something these clubs can't.

Through the exposure he gets from being part of our set-up, Harry now has his own YouTube channel with well over 200,000 subscribers, from which he can make extra revenue. We can offer these players the platform to do that. Harry and Mike have been involved with the Hashtag United football team too as they are both decent players. I don't think the PSG eSports player is going to be involved in the first-team squad any time soon!

More football teams and YouTubers are getting involved, but obviously it's becoming increasingly expensive to start in it from scratch, so it was good that we got involved early. I'm extremely proud of my eSports team and I love it that we go toe-to-toe with the big clubs. I think it's brilliant that you've got this old world of traditional football, with the likes of Man City and West Ham, overlapping with the new world of YouTube teams like us.

It's become an increasingly big part of what we do, to the point where I even had to miss the 2017 Sidemen match because of a clash with the Ultimate Team Championship Grand Final in Berlin. I was gutted to miss it, but I had to be there to support the Hashtag lads, as well as to perform my commentary duties. Working at the events is a lot of fun. We have a great team made up of legendary eSports-casters Joe

Miller and Leigh 'Deman' Smith, as well as football royalty Jimmy Conrad and FUT expert and streamer ChuBoi.

Ever since I was first introduced to *FIFA* eSports I've been a bit of a fanboy, and I felt that starting my own team would be a fast-track way to owning a club that was the best in the world. Tass's victory in the tournament in Paris was a big step to achieving that, making us the number-one ranked team in the world at the time.

It's funny how things turn out. When I was young, all I was interested in was football and football video games, and that line has followed me throughout my life, with my playing football every week and making *FIFA* videos, to where I am now. With Hashtag I play football for my own club and I run an eSports team. It feels like I'm doing a slightly more grown-up version of everything I was doing as a kid, and that's not a bad feeling at all.

●  ●  ●

It wasn't just the Hashtag eSports players who were getting used to travelling the world to play for the club. We took to the skies with Hashtag United in Division 2 of our real-life *Road to Glory* quest as we played our first match outside of England in Northern Ireland, and we had something special lined up with our American tour.

These away trips were brilliant for building that all-important quality, chemistry, and I think the American tour in particular was where I had to stop a minute and think about just how insane this was. We were taking an amateur football team of 22 players and staff to travel around the USA on the kind of pre-season tour you read about Premier League teams doing. You definitely didn't get this in Sunday league.

The US tour was sponsored by Coca-Cola, a brand so huge they're more used to partnering with FIFA to sponsor trophies like the World Cup. Seb put the deal together with them and they were great, giving us complete creative freedom to make what we wanted to. When working with brands, I find it always works better if they're empowering you to do something you want to make, rather than coming to you with their own idea and a chequebook, and we've been lucky enough to have that relationship with brands like EE and *Top Eleven*, and now Coca-Cola.

Taking an amateur team on tour came with one very big issue, of course. All the lads have jobs and their own commitments and, while the tour wouldn't cost them any money, it would mean taking time off work and leaving families behind for the week, which was much harder for some than for others. Some people, understandably, couldn't make it. I'd never expected us to have to make these kind of demands on their time.

But the spirit we'd built in the squad after everything we'd been through together meant that plenty of the team were more than up for it. They were fully invested in what we were doing, and they didn't want to miss a minute of it.

Part of the motivation for starting this whole thing in the first place was to see more of my mates, and by this stage I was probably seeing them even more than I had been at school! Traditionally, football teams tend to finish up when people hit their mid to late twenties as we all had, and people have kids and get married and generally start taking their responsibilities more seriously, but Hashtag United was keeping us together. The wives and girlfriends – the HashWags – no doubt hated me for constantly taking people away from newborn children and families, and now I was stealing them off to America.

Unbelievably, our top goal-scorer Dan Brown was expecting a child while we were away, but that wasn't going to stop him coming. He would fly out for the first bit of the trip and return home before we went to New York so he could be there for the birth of his baby ... or so he hoped! There are no guarantees where this sort of thing is concerned, and there was a chance he would miss it.[5]

And his strike partner Ryan Adams came to me with an even bigger problem shortly before the tour. Ryan is a self-employed carpenter, which meant that taking the time

---

[5] The good news is that he made it back in time. His daughter Halle Brown is already lined up to be the captain of the first ever Hashtag women's team.

off work to come on tour would be even more difficult for him, as he doesn't get paid when he doesn't work. There's no holiday pay for the self-employed. Added to that, he'd just had a kid too, so he had bigger family commitments at home. He was coming anyway though, until the eve of the tour, when some mug broke into his van and stole all his tools and gear.

Ryan was gutted, obviously, but he told me he couldn't afford to have the time off and replace his gear as well, so he'd have to miss the tour. We were gutted too, and not just because of the goals and assists we'd be missing out on. I got the Chairman on the blower to see what he could do to help.

The Chairman got in touch with TradePoint, who sorted Ryan out with a £2,500 voucher. I surprised him with it and we did a kind of *Supermarket Sweep* trip to the store and bought some new tools, which meant he could make it to America after all.

It was amazing to be able to use what we were doing on YouTube to turn such a negative into a positive for Ryan. Because of the viewers we have, we're in a position where companies like TradePoint want to work with us, so we have you guys watching and supporting us to thank for that too. Being able to do things like this makes us feel like we're part of a family, and that within this family we're part of the wider community on YouTube. It's incredible.

That's what makes us a bit different from your standard football team. Ryan is without doubt one of our better players. He could probably go elsewhere and play to a higher standard than he gets with Hashtag, but he wouldn't have us and the wider YouTube community there to help. He wouldn't have 50,000 followers on Instagram and the taste of recognition that playing in front of hundreds of thousands on YouTube each week offers.

The US trip was a fantastic experience, both in terms of building camaraderie in the squad and opening us up to new experiences. We played at the training ground of brand-new Major League Soccer team Atlanta United against a staff team, including former USA and Fulham player Carlos Bocanegra. We also went to watch the Atlanta United first team play in their packed stadium against Chicago Fire, which was just incredible.

And, speaking of new experiences, I managed to bag a hat-trick out there too. Well, sort of. In our game against the Coca-Cola team, I scored what many call the 'perfect hat-trick' as I got a goal with my left foot, right foot and my head, although one of them was a pretty calamitous own goal. I think it was Faisal 'Manjdog' Manji who christened it the 'imperfect hat-trick', and I'll take that! Even scoring more than once in a game was new territory for me in a Hashtag shirt.

The team were turned out differently for the US tour as we finally had our bespoke Hashtag kits made by Umbro. The kits were something special, made to the same specification as a Premier League football kit, with that snug fit loved by the top players. Thank God I'd carried on my fitness work after my 28th birthday!

We had an away kit made too, which was in the original colours of the Hashtag seven-a-side team Faisal and I had started years before. Twitter is a useful tool for us, and we tweeted a little teaser of the kit before it landed to gain some interest. It was amazing to have been part of the design process and to see the kits in the flesh. We were really happy with them.

We sell the kits in our online store, but we're mindful of how expensive football kits are for young people. We're not going to charge what a Premier League football club would, despite the shirts being of identical quality and having the same production costs, so we try to make them affordable for our fans. I love the idea of a kid wearing the Hashtag kit kicking a ball around in his local park or back garden.

The kit wasn't the only new addition to the side, either. We used Twitter leading up to the tour to give a teaser of a new player we had signed, giving a little bit of a reveal each time. The player was another YouTuber, Charlie Morley. Our fans had been talking about him for a long time and he was a great addition to the squad.

There is a strategy, of course, behind our tweets, the timing of them and the way we share things such as the kit and a new signing. We don't want to be boring and just flatly announce these things. We want to do it in the most creative way possible and offer stories with which our audience can engage, and we want to time these things right, not just get them done at the last minute.

And they are all part of a broader strategy we have for Hashtag in which we don't want to stand still and just rest on our laurels. That's why we did the Hashtag Academy trials, where we invited our viewers to enter a competition to find a new player for the team. We had 20,000 people enter to earn the right to join me and my mates in the team. We've been living our dream, and it seemed only fair that our audience should have the chance to join us in that.

That series was so successful that we didn't only discover one new player, but a handful of talented lads, and a whole new Hashtag Academy team has now been created. We want to keep moving and improving, adding to the squad and the experience all the time and seeing where it takes us.

• • •

My dad always told me that if you want to make a successful business in the long term, it has to be able to work without you. Otherwise you will work yourself to the bone, and having you on top of everything will actually end up limiting its growth.

Fine. That all made sense. But how on earth am I going to do that when I'm in all the videos?

I have heeded his advice as far as I can. I have Alex and my brothers, Seb and Saunders, involved now, taking on a lot of the work I do off-camera. With those guys involved, and with my dad on physio duties for Hashtag and my mum even helping out from time to time, it feels like a real and very modern form of family business.

And with Hashtag United, the unthinkable will happen one day. There will come a point when I have to hang up my boots, whether that's because I'm no longer good enough to get in the team (and you can insert your own joke here about not being good enough right now!) or because age has caught up with me. I'm relatively old by YouTube standards, but I'm probably in my prime by football-player standards; as I got into the game late I'm still convinced I'll be hitting my peak some time in my late thirties!

When the time comes, I will move upstairs – I'm confident the Chairman will find a suitable role for me – and the club will carry on. Because Hashtag is about more than me.

It was always my dream to own a football club. It was just something I imagined I'd do when I was much older and had the means to do so, but we are way ahead of that. Hashtag wasn't created to make money; it was always a passion project. What we've got is pretty special, and I believe the possibilities are limitless.

With the audience we attract, we are way beyond our means in terms of the level of football we play. We have more people watching our games than some fully established professional clubs, yet we are outside the traditional footballing structure. We are nothing to do with the Football Association or FIFA, and I think that scares some people.

I think the old guard get annoyed by the fact that we're getting sponsors and big audiences while not playing by their rules and not giving them a penny, but why should we? They don't own football. They may think they do but they really don't. If you look at the mess institutions like FIFA have got mixed up in, with controversial World Cups in Russia and Qatar, corruption scandals and its status as a non-profit organisation despite having billions in the bank, you have to wonder why we'd even want to march to the beat of their drum.

Beyond our video-game inspired divisions structure, who knows what the future holds for the club. Maybe one day we will join the FA and try to be a team playing in a traditional league. Maybe Hashtag winning the 2033 Premier League trophy isn't quite as ludicrous as it sounds. After all, if Leicester City can do it . . .

But right now I fear that the minute we do that, we become like every other one of the 92-plus professional football clubs in England. And right now we are having more fun making our own path.

We have a different model for a football club, and I think it's much more interesting if we celebrate the things in football that aren't currently celebrated. We want to be part of a newer, more progressive and diverse form of football for the modern fan, more reflective of the audience we enjoy on YouTube.

The kind of club we are means that we can do the things that those in the traditional leagues can't. The essence of the beautiful game isn't broke, so we don't need to rip up the rules and start again, but we can look at bringing in things that fans genuinely want to see because we're not hindered by these old and slow institutions.

It's easy to forget that football starts with passion. It's the love of the game that sees people turning out for Sunday league sides all over the country, that sees people travel for miles to watch their team, no matter how bad they are, and has young people turning on in their millions to watch things like the Wembley Cup.

And for me, playing for Hashtag with the mates I've been playing with for years is all about keeping that love alive.

# 11

# LOVE AND HATE

When I finished university my dad took me for some food at Pizza Hut in Reading. I only had a few hundred subscribers on YouTube, and my future stretching out in front of me felt like a blank canvas. I remember thinking it was quite a pivotal moment in my life, and I was keen to get some good old-fashioned fatherly wisdom from Stevie CB. Between mouthfuls of pizza I asked him generic questions about what the main things were that he'd learned along the way and what advice he could give me as a young man about to take on the world.

Then I got a bit more specific. I was dabbling in things like stand-up comedy and radio, pursuits that, if they worked out, had the potential to bring me a level of acclaim and recognition. I was fairly certain my football 'career' wasn't going anywhere. I wanted to gauge my dad's thoughts on someone pursuing a line of work that could lead to a life with less privacy and more attention than the average person. I asked him, 'Would you rather have everyone in the world know who you are, with half of the world loving you and the other half hating you, or just a hundred people know who you are, but they all love you?'

My dad answered in a heartbeat. 'I'll take the hundred that love me, thanks,' he said.

I just couldn't get my head around it. *The whole world would know who you are!* And yes, half of them might hate you, but I didn't really think that would apply to me. Surely if you behaved in a way that you didn't think was deserving of hate, you'd be fine?

Fast-forward a good few years to today, and a lot has changed – and I'm not just talking about my dietary habits. The whole world clearly doesn't know who I am, but my subscribers now number in the millions so I haven't only got that hundred people who all love me, either. And I have learned that, no matter what you do and how you behave, it is not going to stop people deciding they don't like you, no matter how unwarranted it may be. Especially when they have their anonymity to hide behind on social media.

We have a lot of young viewers, and we'll get tweets from kids wearing a Hashtag shirt that their mum's bought them and it makes me really proud to think that this thing I've created from nothing is now making a little kid happy. It reminds me of when I was their age and I got my first West

Ham shirt. If I've made anyone as happy as that made me, then it's definitely made my day.

Sadly, we've learned from experience that I can't really retweet that sort of thing, even if the tweets ask me to. What should be a nice moment for a kid and their parents, having me acknowledge that and share it with my wider fanbase, can often end up in unnecessary and utterly hateful abuse from a small but venomous minority of people. Some of the stuff we get from Twitter trolls is just despicable.

I think that's what stings the most sometimes about the haters. Yes, by all means, have a pop at me – I get no end of stick about how average I am at football (that's kind of the point, guys) and far more poisonous comments on top of that, and I'm used to it by now – but don't do it to someone who isn't putting themselves out there for this kind of vitriol.

I had to warn the other Hashtag players very early on that they would need to develop thick skins if they were going to put up with the abuse on Twitter and in the comments below the videos, and it obviously affects some more than others. The best thing, of course, is simply to ignore it and not respond to any of it but, as our match against Palmers proved, it's one thing knowing it and quite another acting in this way. We definitely shouldn't have responded to provocation.

It's a sad reality that we have to face but, to borrow a quote from Batman, some people just want to watch the world burn.

I feel sorry for them, really. A highlight of their day is targeting someone, often a person who's done nothing wrong, and trying their best to make them feel bad. I mean, that's a pretty sad existence, isn't it? The truth is that often some of these trolls are actually kids themselves and they probably aren't having a great time in their own life, so they decide to pick on others. It's classic schoolyard bullying, really. The difference is that social media allows them to compete for retweets to see who can be the best bully in the world.

Sometimes I don't think sites like Twitter or YouTube do enough to stamp out this sort of behaviour, but it's so hard to police. Ultimately, as long as people have fake usernames to hide behind, this sort of thing will continue. Particularly in the UK we have a habit of trying to knock people down when they do something with their life. I've never really understood it myself, but I've come to accept it.

It's not just on Twitter and in the YouTube comments that I've encountered this sort of behaviour, either. I wouldn't class myself as famous – last time I checked there were definitely no paparazzi outside the front door – but in certain gaming and football environments I do get recognised.

In 2016 I was vlogging all my West Ham games and I've even been lucky enough to have done a few things with the club, such as introduce them to the world of eSports and host their kit launch at the new stadium. The latter was spectacularly badly timed, as it was around the same time that the club made Tony Carr redundant. He ran the club's academy and brought through amazing players like Rio Ferdinand and Frank Lampard.

I did the kit launch because the original presenter, a reasonably well-known reality star and West Ham supporter, pulled out at the last-minute, and I got a lot of stick for it because some of the older audience didn't like the idea of a YouTuber presenting their team's kit launch. It didn't matter to them that I had a track record in presenting this sort of thing; for them a YouTuber is a catch-all term, a signifier of a new era that they don't feel comfortable in, so they decided to target me.

They'd be much more happy with other West Ham fans from mainstream media presenting the event, like Mark Wright or Ben Shephard. Now, no disrespect to those guys, but what makes them more suitable than me? Is it because they appear in a 40-inch box in your living room instead of on a laptop screen or on a phone?

On top of that, people gave me a load of stick for the club supposedly treating me better than they did an academy legend, as if somehow the two were related and they'd had to choose between keeping Tony Carr and getting me in to do the kit launch. 'Sorry, Tony, we're going to have to let you go because we've got Spence in to host our kit launch for free … '

It made no sense but, like a lot of online abuse, the trolls don't let the facts get in the way of a good smear campaign.

The truth was that a lot of West Ham fans were annoyed, not just at the Tony Carr situation but also at the lack of transfer activity that summer and the recent move from our beloved Boleyn Ground. There was a lot of negativity among the West Ham faithful and, for some reason, a few decided to aim it at me. Off the back of the kit launch I got plenty of hate, and not just from people hiding behind Twitter and live-stream comments.

I went out to Slovenia and Romania for West Ham's Europa League away matches, and I got a fair bit of stick from West Ham fans. Alex was with me, and she got plenty of abuse too, which was really out of order and unwarranted, and someone even tried to start a fight with me. I just didn't get it. I've never received a penny from West Ham, despite what some people think, and I'm a fan who just wants the best for the club.

The Romania game in particular, where we, the away fans, were kept in a cage, was a really bad experience, and at one point after I'd done my vlog, I had a run-in with a 'fan' and thought, *I'm going to get my head kicked in here …*

I stuck up for myself (verbally, at least!), and thankfully the situation didn't get out of hand, but it made me think I shouldn't have gone to the game. It just wasn't worth it. I'm a lifelong West Ham fan, always will be, and a season-ticket holder. I love the club, but I definitely won't be in a hurry to travel to some of these away games in future. It probably put Alex off going to football as well, which is a real shame.

Believe it or not, I also need to be careful when I'm playing football. The match against Palmers showed how necessary it was for me not to respond to physical provocation – a couple of players definitely singled me out and were looking for a reaction – and it means that, as much as I'd love to, it's not so easy for me to just go and play seven- or five-a-side somewhere local in a league any more. I've had to wind that down.

I've had people target me in these kind of games, too. I'm not a shrinking violet and I will react if someone does it on the pitch. Maybe not physically every time – but certainly verbally. In one match I had a guy repeatedly grabbing my neck, like he was trying to choke-slam me, and I said something to the ref. When the player did it for a third time and the ref did nothing, I just pushed the guy to the floor, as I think a lot of people would.

When I looked up, I could see someone filming me. If he'd put that clip up online, and edited it in a certain way, it could have made me look like the bad guy, and I realised it just wasn't worth it. I wasn't safe in that environment so I needed to take myself out of it.

Now, before you start saying, 'Poor Spencer,' and playing the world's smallest violin for me, I do, of course, need to mention the other group from the conversation with my dad. The people who love and support what we do.

Thankfully, they make up the majority of the comments and tweets we receive. I always say that I make content for the modern-day football fan. If you like football and you like eSports and gaming, and you're able to embrace the future of football and have fun finding out what that looks like, then hopefully you should find something to love on my channel, whether you're 14 or 40.

The majority of feedback we get is overwhelmingly positive. I get people of all ages – parents, young kids, teenagers, even older people – leaving lovely words online and approaching me to tell me they enjoy what we're doing. That's amazing to me, engaging the new generation of football fans and having something to offer for the current generation, too. I remember one West Ham fan at that same dodgy game in Romania was from the Israeli West Ham supporters group, and he thanked me for making my match-day vlogs. He said watching them was the closest he could get to going to a game regularly. That's why I do it. Encounters like that always make me feel good.

These are the people we love to hear from. We're not interested in trying to convert people who don't want to embrace change. When we went out to Northern Ireland with Hashtag United, we tweeted out 45 minutes before kick-off that we were in the country to play a match, and 600 people turned up to watch. We even had a pitch invasion at the end! These are the people we want beside us as the football landscape changes so radically.

One of the most surreal moments was when I did a video with Real Madrid star Gareth Bale just after he'd helped Wales qualify for Euro 2016. A load of kids ran over at one point, as you'd expect when one of the world's best players is around ... but instead of running up to Gareth, they all came up to say hello to me.

'Er, guys,' I said, a little sheepishly, 'maybe you hadn't noticed, but Gareth Bale is right over there.'

'Yeah,' they said, 'but he's really famous. You're our mate.'

The power of 'Alright mate, how you doing?' clearly cannot be understated! YouTube has that ability to make us feel like we're in a community rather than an us-and-them situation, and I love that about it. These kids felt like they could approach me as a mate, while to them it was like Bale belonged in a different stratosphere to us (to be fair, Bale belongs in a different stratosphere to most footballers, he's that good).

Some footballers are elevated to the level of a god at times, especially by those of us who see football as a religion. I've been guilty of this. When I went to Camp Nou for Barcelona against Manchester City in the Champions League and saw Leo Messi play live for the first time, all I could think was, *He should be wrapped up in clingfilm in a museum somewhere.*

The concept of Messi actually running around, getting sweaty, muddy, fouled … it just seemed wrong.

I play football with some mates every week, and when I was walking into the hall, a group of teenagers who'd just been playing were coming out, and a couple of them spotted me and asked me for a picture. Cool, no problem at all. When I came out an hour later after playing there they were again, but this time they had a printout of their YouTube channels in their hands. They'd realised I wasn't going anywhere for an hour so they'd gone home, printed some screenshots off and come back to show me their content. I really admire that kind of entrepreneurial spirit, and you never know where it might lead.

I was getting the train into London one day when a young lad came and sat next to me on the bench. He told me he was a fan of my channel and we got talking. I asked him a lot about the kind of content he liked on YouTube. We then sat together on the train and carried on talking – he was a West Ham fan too, so we had plenty to chat about – and when we got off the train I asked him where he was going.

'I'm going for an interview with Jamie Oliver's production company,' he said.

It turned out he'd had some experience as a runner on various shoots, so I said, 'Sweet. Good luck with it, and if it doesn't work out, drop me a message.'

I gave him my details, and three months later when his job with the production company had finished, he hit me up, we went for lunch and I ended up hiring him. His name is Lewis Preston, and you might recognise him from Hashtag matches. He was perfect for us, and he put himself out there to make it happen.

His football prowess had nothing to do with why we hired him, but it was an unexpected bonus. After a few weeks on the job he invited me down for a five-a-side game he was playing in, which I think in hindsight was his secretly putting on a Hashtag United trial for himself. Again, you've got to admire the entrepreneurial spirit.

You've got to back yourself when it comes to these things. You've no idea how often I've been told I'm no good as a footballer, but I've got to back myself when I'm out there playing otherwise – if I believed everything I heard – I'd get mugged off every game. In games for Hashtag or the Wembley Cup, I've been lucky enough to play alongside and against World Cup winners, Champions League winners, Premier League winners, all sorts. If I didn't back myself to at least be able to kick a ball, the mere concept of standing alongside these guys would be enough to send me into hiding!

I backed myself when I left my job with Vincent Kompany, even though everyone told me not to, and I did it again when I left Copa90. When Alex and I were working like mad for a year in our pressure-cooker flat, we were backing ourselves then. If you want to make a success of anything in life, especially on YouTube or something in the creative industry, you need to do it, because you will have to get very used to rejection.

Starting out on YouTube with hardly any views can feel like just one long period of rejection, but it was nothing I hadn't experienced when doing stand-up shows to empty rooms and being passed over for presenting jobs.

You need to have a vision of yourself that you believe is good enough, regardless of what people tell you. Within reason, of course. If you're losing every game at *FIFA* in Division 10 despite having played for years, maybe those dreams of being a pro-*FIFA* player might need to be shelved!

Of course, you always need someone to help you along the way. It's a team game, after all. When I emailed everyone at BigBalls, Rich liked what he saw and gave me the opportunity at We R Interactive. I always try to do the same for anyone with a bit of something about them who gets in touch with me.

And I definitely wouldn't be able to do what I do without the amazing team of people I have around me, especially Alex and my brothers.

I never got into this for fame or money, because no one was getting famous or making money on YouTube when I started out. I got into it because I loved doing it, and that passion for making content has never gone away.

It's probably easy for young people to look at some of the lives on YouTube now and be seduced into thinking what they're seeing is real, and aspire to be like that, to think they can copy it and get the same results. To be fair, I'd probably do the same if I was a kid. But it's not real. It's all a façade. Almost everyone is putting on an act to some degree in their content, so don't be fooled into thinking that's real life. Just like all forms of entertainment, there's a level of interpretation involved.

I was lucky enough to try lots of other things first before I found any success on YouTube, so I had a whole host of influences to draw upon, not just other YouTubers. I had no model to follow, and I just made content I enjoyed and felt strongly about. There is so much great content out there on YouTube now, and you'll find that's the one thing that the best creators on the platform have in common: they feel passionately about what they're doing. They're not just blindly copying someone else in a scramble for subscribers.

I've never gone chasing the money. If I had, I could have stayed working for Vincent Kompany and had a much easier life. I could have gone down the coin-sponsor route or made cheap, low-level content with Alex doing pack-openings in her lingerie if that was what really mattered to me (though she might have had something to say about that … and I know her parents certainly would!).

My way has paid off in the long term. Alex and I have bought a house now, which we never dreamed we'd be in a position to do at our age, but almost everything else we've made has been put straight back into the videos. Because that's what it's all about for me. Coming up with ideas and making them happen – producing content I love and that I hope my viewers will too.

If I had that conversation in Pizza Hut with my dad now, what would I say? I'd definitely understand his point of view, with some of the haters I've encountered both online and in the flesh. But you can't let these people grind you down, and I think I'm in a pretty good position to say that where I am now isn't a bad place to be at all.

I always come back to a quote by the American singer-songwriter Bob Dylan. He said, 'A man is a success if he gets up in the morning and goes to bed at night, and in between he does what he wants to do.'

I'm lucky enough to be able to say that's me. I'm living my dream, spending my days playing my favourite games and taking part in football matches all over the world with my mates, despite being nowhere near good enough. And you, our readers, subscribers and viewers, are the ones making that all possible. You're helping us make our dreams come true, and I'm unbelievably grateful for that. Together, we're changing the game.

# FULL-TIME: DROP A LIKE

Thanks for reading, guys, and I hope you enjoyed it. I'd ask you to drop a like or subscribe, but given that we're in good old-fashioned book format here, it just leaves me to say: until next time. I'll see you when you're older. Don't go changing. Oh, and don't forget to hashtag it!

I couldn't possibly finish without thanking some of the key individuals who have made this book, and the crazy adventure that's become my life, possible.

First of all, thanks to my publisher Sara Cywinski for giving me the freedom to do the book my way and for believing in the project from day one. I really appreciate it.

Next, I must thank Steve Burdett. Our long chats often felt like (much-needed) therapy sessions, but without them this book wouldn't exist. Being able to put this together in what has easily been the busiest year of my life was all thanks to

Steve's uncanny ability to take my often random thoughts and put them down onto paper in a much more intelligible form. Cheers Steve, I owe you a drink or three!

Big thanks also to Dave Brown at APE, Anna Mrowiec and the rest of the team at Ebury.

There's a surprising amount of people working behind the scenes in what we do and I could easily write a paragraph about all of them. Apologies if I've forgotten anyone!

I want to offer huge thanks to Lewis Preston, Adam Boultwood, Faisal 'Manjdog' Manji, David Molumby, Glen Cowie, Robbie Morgan, Jack Hoyle, Tom Mallion, Ash Raim and Marius Hjerpseth. All very talented guys whose hard work makes my life so much easier!

Thanks to: Mr Haskett for the being the best teacher I ever had; Sean Baker for giving me my first real chance in football at Heyridge Boys; Greg Osborne for being my university radio co-host and doing the buttons; Richard Welsh for seeing something in me and giving me that first leg up after university; Oli Madgett for being a great first boss and the nicest man you'll ever meet; Tom Thirlwall for believing in a weird idea about a man playing *FIFA* in a mask and giving me the perfect opportunity to learn my trade; Vincent Kompany, Klaas Gaublomme and Vincent Jansen for giving me some amazing experiences and one of the best jobs imaginable; Matt Roberts, Nick Farnhill, the rest of the Poke team and everyone at EE who have made the Wembley Cup possible and so memorable – thanks for giving me the best night of my life; *Top Eleven* and Umbro for believing in our crazy idea about a football team named after a keyboard symbol; Brent Koning at EA for trusting me to be one of the faces of his *FIFA* eSports revolution; every single player that's ever put on a Hashtag United shirt and gone into battle with me; the Hashtag United eSports players for doing us proud and leading us into the future.

Now, just like in most acknowledgements, I need to thank my family. However, in my case I owe my family more thanks than most do.

My older brother Seb has allowed us to take everything up a level since he came on board and his constant support and hard work have been invaluable to everything we do together. We've come a long way since battling it out on *FIFA 98*. Thanks for everything, Sebby boy, long may it continue.

My younger brother Saunders doesn't get the credit he deserves, but chances are if you're watching one of my videos and you think it looks good or well-edited, it's probably down to him! He's super talented and I can't wait to see what he does with the rest of his career. No doubt whatever it is, it will be spectacular. Saundie Daundie, you're a legend. Thanks for being so great at what you do!

My mum Sindy and my dad Steve are the best parents a lad could ask for; they're always there for me whenever I need them and they've given me all of their support and backing from day one (even when my decisions probably didn't make sense to them at the time).

If you went to the Wembley Cup in 2016 you probably heard my mum screaming at the top of her voice. Mum, you are the best person I know and I love you all the way to Bell House and back. Thank you.

As for my dad, aka Stevie CB, the physio of dreams, he's so much more than Hashtag's medical man. Dad, you're my hero and I hope I end up half the man you are. Thanks for always being there.

Having all of my family involved in the projects we take on now is the icing on the cake for me. It makes everything so much sweeter. We're a family and we're a team, and a pretty damn good team if I do say so myself.

Most of all, though, I have to thank my partner in crime, Alex. Alex, the role you've played in all of this cannot be over-exaggerated. The risk you took in leaving your job to follow my crazy dream was a catalyst for so much of what's happened since, and I hope you know how grateful I am for all of the hard work you've put in to help us achieve what we have. Football was never your passion but you made it your life in order to let me do things I never thought were possible. Not only were you the key to all of this, but there's no one else in the world I'd rather have done it with. Considering we spend so much of our lives together it's amazing that you're not sick of the sight of me yet, but I love you now more than ever and I'm so lucky that my university bedroom got that leak back in 2007. Thank you for being the most patient, understanding, considerate, giving and breathtakingly beautiful woman in the world.

Finally, I have to thank all of you, the readers, the viewers, the hashtaggers, the legends on the other side of the screen who have changed my life. Without the incredible support that you've given me over the years on YouTube, none of this would ever have happened. I'm eternally grateful for the situation you've put me and my family in, and I will continue to do everything I can to make the sort of content you deserve. I hope you've enjoyed reading the story about how it all unfolded for me, but please know that regardless of the decisions I made, without you watching my videos then none of it would have mattered. I hope that over the next few years I can create a whole load of new memories for us to reminisce about and ponder over in the future. The best is yet to come – got to save some stuff for the sequel! After all, you know I love a series.

Don't go changin'.

Your mate,

Spencer FC